# THE BOTANICAL ATLAS

THE

BOTANICAL

ATLAS.

# THE BOTANICAL ATLAS

*A Guide to the Practical Study of Plants*

**Daniel McAlpine**

Introduction by

**Dr. S. M. Walters**

SMITHMARK

Previously published in 1883 by W. & A. K. Johnston,
Edinburgh

Copyright © this edition 1989 Studio Editions

This edition published in 1996
by SMITHMARK Publishers,
a division of U.S. Media Holdings, Inc.,
16 East 32nd Street, New York, NY 10016.

SMITHMARK books are available for bulk purchase
for sales promotion and premium use.
For details write or call the manager of special sales,
SMITHMARK Publishers, 16 East 32nd Street,
New York, NY 10016; (212) 532-6600.

Produced by Studio Editions,
an imprint of Random House UK Ltd,
20 Vauxhall Bridge Road, London SW1V 2SA.

ISBN 0-8317-7495-9

Printed and bound in Singapore

10 9 8 7 6 5 4 3 2 1

**Publisher's Note**

As Dr Walters' Introduction explains, *The Botanical Atlas* is a
remarkable product of late Victorian scientific educational
literature. The facsimile that we present has an explanatory
text for each of the 53 plates reproduced *verbatim.*
Inevitably, botanical scholarship in the intervening century
has advanced to a varied extent. In general the greatest
advances in knowledge have occurred in the smallest of the
'Lower Plants' so that the Cryptogams appear more dated
than other areas of botanical work. At the other extreme it
could be said that, with relatively little change to some

# CONTENTS

# INTRODUCTION

This remarkable example of Victorian book production can be appreciated at two levels. The full-page illustrations speak for themselves, from the microscopic enlargement of the speck-like *Volvox* (Cryptogams, Plate IX) to the fascinating detail of the Plate (Phanerogams, Plate V) devoted to the Martagon Lily and the Crown Imperial. They can be studied as minor works of art, impressive both for the skill and care of the original artists. But they are much more than that: they represent the flowering of what is recognisably modern botany which the late Victorian educational expansion brought in its train, and it is the background to this story that we must first sketch in.

The history of botanical science can be traced back to the teachings of Aristotle and his pupil Theophrastus in Ancient Greece, and this venerable tradition is obvious to the present day in that, by international agreement, we use classical, Latin- or Greek-based names for all plants (and animals). Fascinating though these classical roots are, we must confine ourselves for the present purpose to the briefest mention of botany over nearly 2000 years from the time of Aristotle to the rise of what is recognisably modern science in Europe in the seventeenth century. Risking a broad generalization, we can say that throughout this stretch of the Christian era what botany there was flourished as a handmaid of medicine. The struggle to break away from the 'herbal' tradition and to observe and to study plants for their own sake is epitomized in Britain, as elswhere in Europe, by the history of Botanic Gardens.

Originally institutions devoted very largely to the cultivation of medicinal plants, they gradually emerged from this restriction in the seventeenth and eighteenth centuries and took on their modern shape. In the case of Edinburgh, where our book originated, this history is excellently told in the book by Fletcher and Brown, 'The Royal Botanic Garden, Edinburgh' published in 1970 to commemorate the tercentenary of this famous Garden. In London the remarkable Chelsea Physic Garden, also more than 300 years old, can still be visited and its collections admired on its original site by the river in Chelsea. (The dominance of Kew over Chelsea and indeed all other Botanic Gardens is a late eighteenth and nineteenth-century phenomenon.)

The pioneers of empirical, observational and experimental botany were, in Britain, men like John Ray (1627-1705) who were Fellows of the newly-formed Royal Society, and the complex history of our subject unfolds over three centuries. A glance at the second half of our book, devoted to 'Phanerogams', mainly what we would commonly call 'Flowering Plants', reminds us that one strand of accurate observation developed early. This concerned the detailed description of the structures of flowers and fruits. In spite of fundamental advances undreamt of by Ray in the seventeenth century or the great Swedish naturalist Linnaeus in the eighteenth, which would make much of what is studied in a modern Department of Botany totally incomprehensible to those great botanists, the basic comparative morphology of the flower remains unaltered from the eighteenth century. The original wall-diagrams (see below) from which the illustrations of the flowers of Sage (*Salvia*) are taken (Phanerogams, Plate XXIII) are, for example, usable in any lecture on the adaptations of flowers for insect pollination, as I know from my own teaching experience.

What then has changed, and why? The changes all refer to Part I of the book, devoted to the Cryptogams, or 'Lower Plants' as we still commonly call them. In nearly all general botanical works up to 1840, very little of the text was devoted to the 'Lower Plants', for the reason that an elucidation of their structural relationships to each other and to the Flowering Plants could not be made until better microscopes were available. The old-fashioned term 'Cryptogam', meaning in Greek 'hidden union', refers to this lack of knowledge of the details of their reproductive processes. By 1883, when our book first appeared, this revolutionary advance had happened, and an exciting new evolutionary picture of the whole Plant Kingdom and its essential unity of basic structure is presented here, for the first time, to British students in English. Cryptogams, Plate XXVI and the accompanying text set out the whole story, which was almost entirely the product of Germanic scholarship mainly in the new scientifically and technologically-minded Universities which sprang up and flourished in Germany between the end of the Napoleonic Wars and the foundation of a unified German State in 1871. An excellent account of this important period in the history of botany is available in the later chapters of Professor A. G. Morton's 'History of Botanical Science' (1981) — a book, incidentally, written in Edinburgh by a man whose breadth of knowledge is, as so often, a tribute to Scottish education.

This total supremacy of German botany is, of course, part of a much wider cultural and scientific phenomenon of the Victorian period, and the story cannot be told here. Perhaps it is sufficient to remind the curious reader that much of the impetus which underlay the British industrial and scientific drive in the late Victorian period came *via* the personal dedication of the German Prince Albert, Prince Consort to Queen Victoria, who was committed to a vision of rational scientific and technological progress involving wide popular education. It is impossible to understand the shape of British science if this crucial influence is ignored. So far as botany is concerned, it soon became obvious to the brighter students attracted to plant studies that a period of study in a German University under one of the great Professors — among them, De Bary (Strasburg), von Nägeli (Munich), Pringsheim (Berlin), Sachs (Würzburg) and Strasburger (Jena) — was a necessary part of their education. By 1872, however, when Thomas Henry Huxley transferred his science department (originally the Royal School of Mines and Science) to South Kensington, modern German-style biology was being taught in English in an atmosphere of intellectual excitement difficult for us to recapture. Here Huxley, the zoologist, and Thiselton-Dyer and Vines, the botanists, were producing a new generation of biologists to teach their science in the new National Schools introduced after the Education Act of 1870. This new curriculum was explicitly evolutionary, presenting the range of plants and animals from the lowest unicellular forms to the flowering plants and man himself in terms of common ground-plans against an evolutionary time-scale. Nothing has essentially changed in the way we teach elementary biology of organisms today — if we still teach any: what the twentieth century has seen is an enormous increase in what is now usually distinguished as 'cell biology', until there is real danger that comparative studies of anatomy and morphology drop out of the modern University syllabus.

Against this background we can understand the author of our book and his contribution to botanical education. Born in Ayrshire, Scotland, in 1848, he studied botany in London under Huxley and Thiselton-Dyer, and returned to Scotland to lecture at Heriot Watt College in Edinburgh in 1877. He held this post for seven years, and during this period produced the two major related works which interest us. 'The Botanical Atlas' is the derivative product of his earlier work entitled 'Anatomical and Physiological Atlas of Botany', which needs some explanation. One of the educational by-products of German botanical scholarship was the publication of sets of large 'wall-diagrams' (Wandtafeln) for use in the lecture-room. Most British University Departments of Botany dating from the period before the first World War probably had at least one of these sets. In my own Department I have used these excellent diagrams occasionally, realising that they combined clarity, size and accuracy to an unrivalled extent. Such diagrams must have been an integral part of the teaching received by the young McAlpine, and in 1880 he arranged for a famous set to be published by Johnston's of Edinburgh, together with three small 'Handbooks' in which he gave an edited text in English to accompany each diagram. In the 'Preface to the English edition' he states:

'In translating the text I have endeavoured to make it serviceable for all classes of students by adopting such technical terms as are met with in the best modern works, and by giving the "English literature" alone under each subject.'

The literature cited includes as appropriate works by Charles Darwin, T. H. Huxley and others, as also Sachs' 'Text-book of Botany' recently translated into English. The Preface to '*The Botanical Atlas*' explains the relation to this earlier publication, in paying tribute to the author of the original German edition, Professor Dodel-Port, of the University of Zurich, 'who allowed me free and full use of the beautiful figures.' A detailed comparison of the two works confirms, however, that much of the 'Botanical Atlas', though interestingly derivative in origin, represents the talents of a brilliant and inspired young lecturer, McAlpine himself.

Daniel McAlpine's later career was in Australian Universities, where he became widely known as a specialist in mycology and fungus diseases of commercial crop plants. He died in Victoria in 1932.

Dr. S. M. WALTERS
University Botanic Garden
Cambridge
12 · 1 · 1989

# PREFACE

This work is intended as a guide to the practical study of Flowering Plants—and to this end selected types of the principal Natural Orders are dissected, drawn, and briefly described. Practical work requires to be *encouraged* for we have been so long accustomed to obtain our knowledge of Nature entirely through the agency of books, that the "book of Nature" has become to many the printed page and not the living reality. The inducements here offered are—the selection of Common Forms; the Dissection of Parts in their regular order, usually with just sufficient detail to illustrate their leading characteristics; the Drawings in their natural colour, for ready comparison with the natural object; and the necessary Explanation opposite of what is seen and how to see it.

In using this book the Student may either practically examine the forms figured or their equivalents—thus, the Shepherd's Purse may be chosen instead of the Wall-flower; the Garden Pea instead of the Sweet Pea, and so on. He may then examine, with less detail, other Plants belonging to the same Natural Order, noting chiefly peculiarities or differences. Some may take exception to many of the examples, on the ground that they are already sufficiently illustrated in the ordinary Text-books; but it may suffice to point out that, even in two such common forms as Buttercups and Daisies, careful examination will reveal new features of interest. Thus, the Buttercup shows beautifully the gradual passage of the *compound* Foliage-leaves into the *simple*, green Floral-leaves or Sepals; and the Daisy will be found to exhibit occasionally the Five-lobed Corolla and the Five-lobed Stigma, although it is invariably figured as having two only in each case.

It will be observed that the Flower and its various parts passing into fruit and Seed are mainly considered in the Volume; and the Leaves are merely introduced, copied from Nature, for purposes of comparison with the Floral-leaves. This forms the best introduction to a course of Practical Botany, since the eye and hand trained to dissect and distinguish these comparatively conspicuous structures, then can more readily pass to the consideration of Root and Stem and Leaf, and their minute structure. In the next Volume the minuter forms of Plant Life are dealt with, where niceties of manipulation and the use of the highest powers of the microscope are required.

The style of Botany that is too much the fashion at present, and the kind of Botany which it is the purpose of this Work to encourage, are strikingly shown, in a recent Report by the Examiner in Botany for the Science and Art Department, who says:-

'The candidates have displayed a good deal of knowledge, but as far as I can see if is of a purely literary kind. It has been obtained from books and not from study of the objects themselves. The result is the exhibition of much confusion of ideas which could scarcely have arisen if the candidates had ever attentively examined the things they have written about.'

DANIEL M<sup>C</sup>ALPINE

EDINBURGH, *December 1882*

# CRYPTOGAMS

PLATE I.

# GLŒOCAPSA, OSCILLATORIA, SCYTONEMA, RIVULARIA, NOSTOC, PALMELLA, EUGLENA, and YEAST.

*(Figs. 1b, 5, and 6a after Luerssen; Figs 3 and 4 after Dr Welwitsch.)*

## GLŒOCAPSA.

Glœocapsa (Gr. *glia,* glue; *capsa,* a case) occurs in damp places, and may be conveniently had for examination from the glass of damp green-houses, here it forms in gelatinous masses.

The single rounded cell consists of a small protoplasmic mass surrounded by a gelatinous cell-wall, and divides in all the directions of space till it forms a little colony. Division takes place within the parent envelope, and each daughter-cell forms for itself a new cell-wall. The original envelope, stretched in this way, absorbs more and more water until, towards the exterior, it gradually shades off into the surrounding liquid.

*Fig. 1a* Examine under highest power: 1*st,* as it naturally occurs; 2*nd,* stained with magenta; and 3*rd,* with iodine to bring out cell-wall distinctly.

The young cell stains deeply, showing the protoplasm to be dense; the next is undergoing division lengthways, and the third shows transverse division.

*Fig. 1b* Showing different stages of division, ending in the formation of a colony.

## OSCILLATORIA.

Oscillatoria (so named from its oscillating or pendulum-like movement) occurs in various situations, either in water or on damp earth; but it may be found at any season of the year by the roadside, where it forms those spreading green patches at the bottom of damp walls, etc.

Under the microscope it is seen to consist of long filaments, each with a distinct colourless sheath of cellulose, containing protoplasm coloured bottle-green. The protoplasmic contents are marked by transverse lines, with alternate lines only faintly indicated. The power of growth is equally distributed over the whole filament, and any one of the segments can divide into two new ones.

Under the influence of light these filaments exhibit movement. They have a slow, swinging movement from side to side, the stiff filament giving the idea of a pendulum in motion.

*Fig. 2a* Mount a small quantity in a drop of water, and examine under highest power.
Long filaments, with their contents divided by numerous transverse lines.
*Fig. 2b* Press upon cover-glass so as to crush the filaments.
The contents are seen to be little discs wrapped in a sheath of cellulose, which lies about to be ruptured.
*Fig. 2c* The faint lines between the more decided transverse markings are the expression of the incipient division of each disc into two.
At the base a single disc is shown.
*Fig. 2d* The moving filament swings from side to side, at the same time going forward.

## SCYTONEMA.

Scytonema (Gr. *skutos,* a whip; *nema,* a thread) occurs usually in dense tufts on moist rocks, sometimes in sufficient quantity to disguise the natural brownish or blackish colour of the rocks. This particular kind is of a shining black colour.

Instead of growth going on regularly throughout the filament, as in Oscillatoria, there are some points at which growth is more vigorous, and this bulging gives rise to side filaments or branches.

*Fig. 3* Shows a small tuft in its natural size.

*Fig. 4* Shows a small filament magnified. There is the common sheath wrapping round the discs, and branches going off at particular spots.

## RIVULARIA.

Rivularia (Lat. *rivulus,* a rill) may be found in mountain streams, coating the surfaces of submerged stones or water-plants.

It forms dark-green cushions, which are often incrusted with carbonate of lime, thus giving the whole a peculiar hardened look.

It departs from the uniform characters exhibited by the plants already considered in several respects. 1. Whereas, in Oscillatoria, the filaments of jointed protoplasm could evidently go on growing to any extent, here growth seems to die out at one end, giving rise to a tapering whip-lash filament. 2. Whereas, in Oscillatoria, the filaments were of equal diameter throughout, here not only is there a tapering at one end of the filament, but there is a globular development at the other end, in the form of a Basal-cell or Heterocyst,

11

incapable of further sub-division. 3. Whereas each segment of Oscillatoria had the power of division, and a detached disc could give rise to a new plant, here certain cells, in the course of a filament, only possess that power. One of the cells becomes a Basal-cell, and the cell immediately above that grows out into a new filament. As the whip ends of the filaments are all directed outwards, there is a radiating appearance presented, with a Basal-cell at the bottom of each filament. 4. The large cell above the Basal-cell may grow till it is fully ten times longer than broad, thus becoming capable of persisting during the winter when the rest of the plant has decayed, and producing a new Rivularia in the spring.

*Fig.* 5 A single filament with Basal-cell    or Heterocyst (Gr. *heteros,* different) at    one end, and pointed cell at the other.

## THE COMMON NOSTOC.

The Common Nostoc is to be looked for after rain, as it readily dries up. It occurs as dark, shapeless, jelly-like masses on garden walks or grass plots.

Under the microscope there is seen to be imbedded in the jelly long convoluted filaments, composed of little globular cells, forming a beautiful beaded neck-lace arrangement, with larger cells every here and there—the Heterocysts. The neck-lace is composed of distinct cells, and not mere discs of protoplasm embedded in a sheath, as in Oscillatoria. The embedding jelly is probably the cell walls softened with excess of water and run together.

The mode of multiplication varies. The portion of the old colony, between two heterocysts, breaks away from the jelly, and in the water the cells stretch themselves transversely and divide repeatedly, *parallel* to the long axis of the chain. In this way a number of short filaments are formed, side by side, which afterwards arrange themselves end to end, and so form the long meandering chain. In rare cases spores are formed generally between two heterocysts, and persisting after the rest of the filament has decayed, they give rise to a new chain.

*6a* Examine small portion of the jelly    chain, with larger cells occurring at    Sulphuric acid to show the cellulose
under highest power, and    intervals.    coat investing each cell.
observe the beautiful twistings of the    *Fig. 6b* Stain with Iodine and

## PALMELLA CRUENTA.

Palmella Cruenta (Gr. *palmos,* a shuddering; Lat. *cruentus,* bloody), or "Gory Dew" occurs towards the bottom of damp walls, and may frequently be observed even in the thoroughfares of towns. It is readily recognised by its bloody hue, and in cold water it yields a beautiful, pale pink colour.

The cells are embedded in gelatinous matter, and are sometimes angular from pressure.

*Fig. 7a, b* Examine, under highest    the walls in flakes, and only a small    mounted for examination.
power, in a drop of water. It peels off    clean speck from the surface need be

## EUGLENA.

Euglena (Gr. *eu,* great ; *glene,* the eye-ball), unlike the preceding, is of a brilliant green hue, yet with a touch of red in it. It occurs commonly in the black water draining from manure heaps, which is known to be rich in Nitrogen.

Euglena is a motile organism, moving freely about by means of a long vibratile cilium, at least the length of the body. It is reckoned by some zoologists as an animal belonging to the Infusoria; but there are many points in its character which bear out its vegetable nature, so that if an animal, it is a vegetating one.

It consists of a spindle-shaped body, tapering at both ends, but as it moves about the outline varies and assumes all possible shapes. There is a red spot, called the eye-spot, towards one end. The contents are distinctly granular and for the most part tinged with the green colouring matter chlorophyll. In the presence of sunlight, oxygen is evolved as a result of the decomposition of carbonic anhydride.

It multiplies by internal division. When about to do so it gradually becomes still and rounded, drops its cilium, and encloses itself in a structureless case or cyst. The contents divide into numerous portions, each of which, on being set free by the rupture of the cyst, becomes a new Euglena.

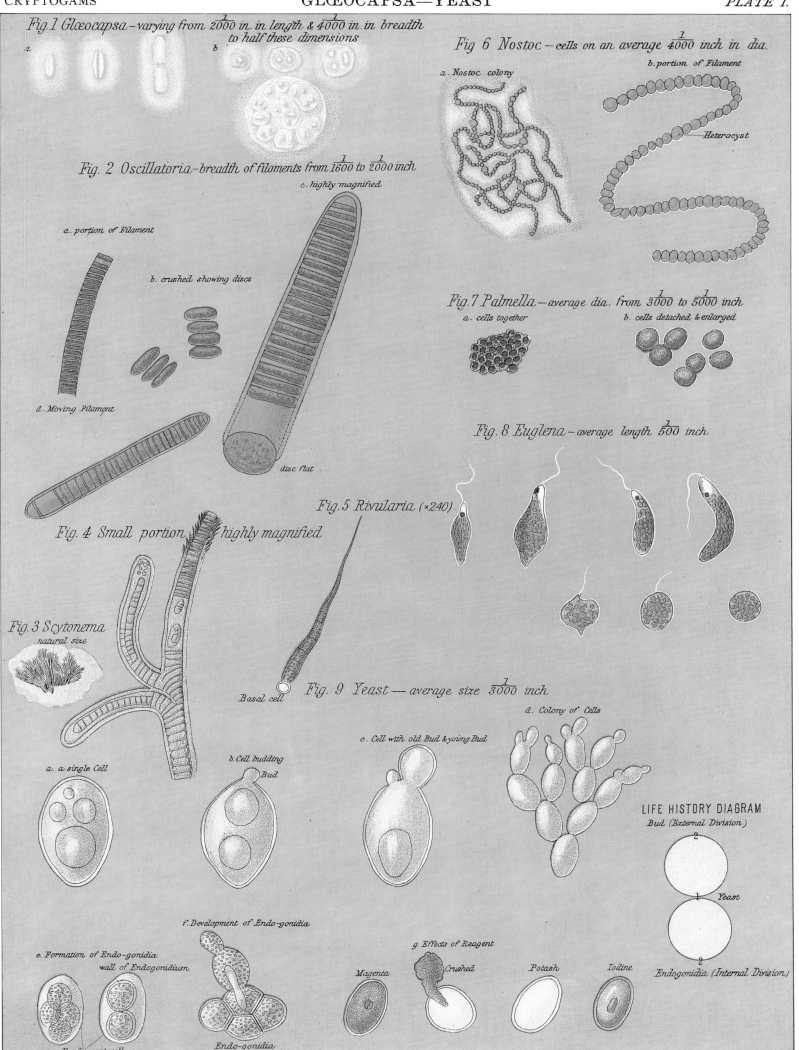

Fig. 1 Glœocapsa – varying from $\frac{1}{2000}$ in. in length & $\frac{1}{4000}$ in. in breadth to half these dimensions

a    b

Fig 6 Nostoc – cells on an average $\frac{1}{4000}$ inch in dia.

a. Nostoc colony      b. portion of Filament

Heterocyst

Fig. 2 Oscillatoria – breadth of filaments from $\frac{1}{1600}$ to $\frac{1}{2000}$ inch

c. highly magnified

a. portion of Filament

b. crushed showing discs

d. Moving Filament

disc flat

Fig. 7 Palmella – average dia. from $\frac{1}{3000}$ to $\frac{1}{5000}$ inch

a. cells together      b. cells detached & enlarged

Fig. 8 Euglena – average length $\frac{1}{500}$ inch

Fig. 5 Rivularia (×240)

Fig. 4 Small portion highly magnified

Fig. 3 Scytonema
natural size

Basal cell

Fig. 9 Yeast — average size $\frac{1}{3000}$ inch

d. Colony of Cells

c. Cell with old Bud & young Bud

b. Cell budding
Bud

a. a single Cell

LIFE HISTORY DIAGRAM
Bud (External Division)

Yeast

f. Development of Endo-gonidia

e. Formation of Endo-gonidia
wall of Endogonidium

g. Effects of Reagent

Magenta    Crushed    Potash    Iodine

Endogonidia (Internal Division)

wall of parent cell

Endo-gonidia

Engraved, Printed and Published by W. & A.K. Johnston, Edinburgh & London.

*Fig. 8* Dip a glass rod into the green scum, and leave the smallest possible portion on a slide, and examine under highest power. This shows the encysted or encysting stage. Examine a drop of the blackish water for the fully developed forms.

They will be seen moving about leisurely and twisting themselves into all conceivable shapes. By the application of iodine, the cilium will be rendered apparent ; and it is curious to note that Euglena is not propelled behind by its cilium but is actually dragged along by it. In the same liquid there will be a variety of organisms, but the red eye-spot will mark out Euglena even when it is rounded and motionless.

## YEAST (Saccharomyces—Lat. *saccharum,* sugar; Gr. *mukes,* fungus).

## Yeast may be obtained at any brewer's establishment.

*Fig. 9a, b, c,* and *d* Take up a little yeast with pipette, and drop on to slide, and examine under highest power. In every position the granules appear round, hence they are not flat, like a coin, but globular. Cell-wall. Protoplasmic contents. Vacuoles filled with cell-sap.

Buds produced, and this process may be repeated, as in *d,* until an aggregation is formed. *Fig. 9e, f* Starve some yeast by laying it out on a piece of plaster-of-Paris, and keep it moist with wet blotting-paper under a bell-jar. Under these circumstances the yeast is unable to throw off buds, so it breaks up internally in about a week into four portions, which have the power of reproducing the yeast under favourable conditions. *Fig. 9g* The vacuole is seen to be less stained than the rest. In the larger cells the staining material may bring out a dark or denser spot, which is the Nucleus.

*Life History*—The Yeast under ordinary circumstances multiplies by budding, and this may go on indefinitely as long as nourishment is supplied, but when nourishment fails, it can divide internally, and so prolong its existence by means of Endogonidia (Gr. *endon,* within ; *gone,* seed).

NOTE—The term *Gonidium* will be used to denote cells non-sexually produced, capable of reproducing the plant. On the other hand, the term *Spore* will be applied to such cells as result from sexual reproduction.

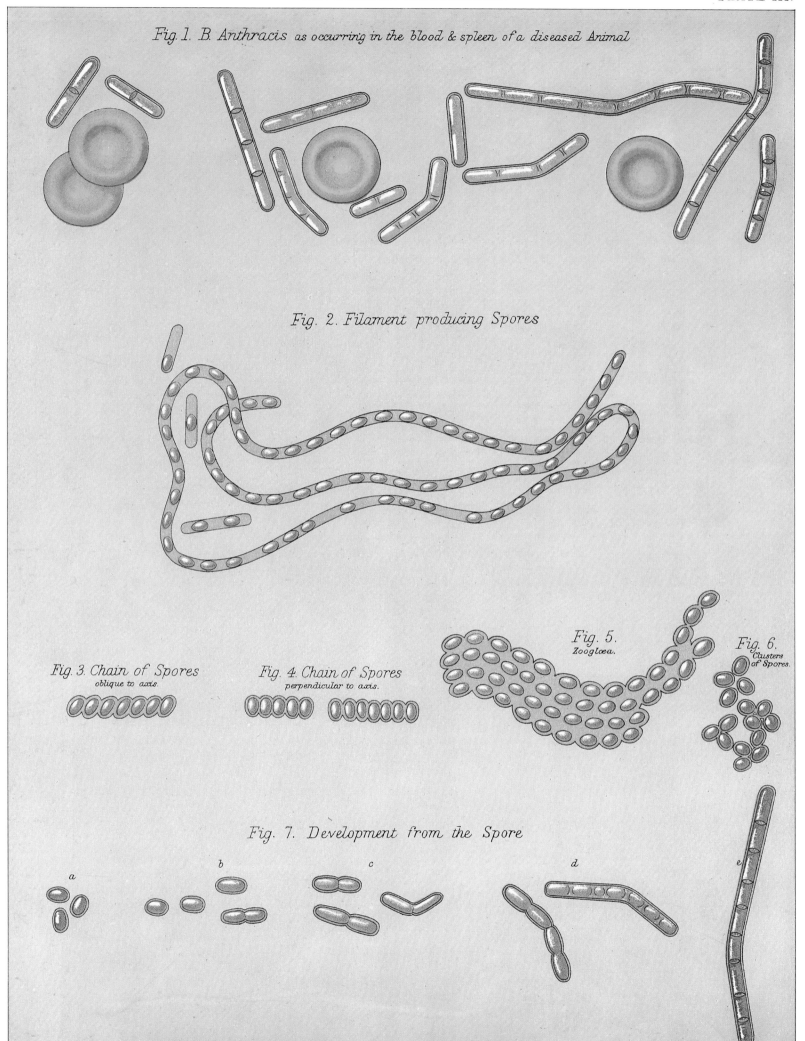

Fig. 1. *B. Anthracis* as occurring in the blood & spleen of a diseased Animal

Fig. 2. *Filament producing Spores*

Fig. 3. *Chain of Spores* oblique to axis.

Fig. 4. *Chain of Spores* perpendicular to axis.

Fig. 5. *Zoogloea.*

Fig. 6. Clusters of Spores.

Fig. 7. *Development from the Spore*

a    b    c    d    e

Engraved, Printed and Published by W. & A.K. Johnston, Edinburgh & London.

PLATE IV.

# PROTOCOCCUS, PANDORINA, ULOTHRIX, and HYDRODICTYON.

## PROTOCOCCUS VULGARIS.

Protococcus Vulgaris (Gr. *protos,* first; *kokkos,* a berry), or Pleurococcus, is well—known as the green scum on the bark of trees. It is so widely diffused that its means of multiplication must be very perfect. In fact it is like a continuous growing point, ever dividing and ever ready to divide.

Under the microscope it is seen to consist of rounded cells, usually having a nucleus. This nucleus is a denser portion of the protoplasm and stains more deeply than the rest. The cells are also seen to be divided into two, three, or four portions. But towards the end of autumn another process of division takes place. The contents of the cell break up into a great number of little masses which, on escaping by the rupture of the cell-wall, are seen to consist of naked bits of protoplasm, with two threads of it propelling them rapidly through the water. This naked moving protoplasm afterwards forms a cell-wall.

*Fig. 1* Take a little bit of the bark of a tree, with this green scum upon it, and scrape off some of it into a drop of water on a slide. Examine under highest power.

(*a.*) Ordinary resting-form consisting of Cell-wall and green-coloured contents.

(*b.*) Iodine brings out Nucleus—seen as a small dark spot in the centre of the cell.

Iodine and Sulphuric acid together— the cell-wall becomes blue and the protoplasm coagulates.

Crushed—to distinguish clearly between the tough cell-wall and the semi-fluid protoplasm.

Potash—dissolving the protoplasm.

(*c.*) Multiplication by Division into four. The protoplasm first of all separates into two masses, and cell-wall forms in the partition between. Next, each half behaves like the original whole so that four divisions are formed. These divisions separate, become rounded, and each forms a new Protococcus.

(*d.*) Endogenous Division producing motile forms. The protoplasmic contents begin to divide in the same way as before, but instead of stopping at four, there is division into numerous segments of naked protoplasm. The particles become rounded and escape as *motile forms* through the rupture of the original case. The motile ciliated forms, non-sexually produced, are called Zoogonidia (Gr. *zoon,* an animal). In the resting-forms it will be noticed, that they were clothed with a cell-wall before *being* set free, whereas the motile forms only assume a cellulose covering afterwards.

*Life History.*—Multiplication takes place either by simple division into four portions, or into numerous motile forms, which afterwards settle down and return to the ordinary resting-form.

## PROTOCOCCUS PLUVIALIS.

Protococcus Pluvialis (Lat. *pluvia,* rain) as the specific name denotes, occurs in places where rain-water collects.

*Fig. 2* Take some of the muddy sediment from rain-water, mount with clean water and examine under highest power.

Observe motionless and motile forms. The motile forms may either be clothed with a wall or naked.

## PANDORINA.

Pandorina (Gr. *Pandora,* a beautiful woman) occurs in ponds and ditches, but it may be had for examination from certain Natural History dealers.

There are sixteen cells united into a free-swimming colony of globular shape by a gelatinous investment. Each of these sixteen cells may give rise to a new colony. The cilia are withdrawn, whereby the whole comes to rest, and each individual divides into sixteen portions like the parent. In other cases, however, a single cell does not reproduce the colony. Two cells from different individuals fuse together and the common mass ultimately forms a young colony. This process is called Conjugation, where the two uniting elements closely resemble each other, and the result of it may be traced in the Figures.

*Fig. 3a* Colony or Cœnobium (Gr. *koine,* in common; *bios,* life) consisting of sixteen cells or Zoogonidia. Each Zoogonidium has a red eye-spot and two projecting cilia, by the collective and harmonious action of them all a rolling motion is imparted to the whole family.

(*b, c*) Male and Female Zoospores. These reproductive cells are produced from different colonies, the smaller being reckoned the Male, and the larger the Female element.

(*d, e*) In conjugation, the two elements first come into contact by their ciliated ends, then they gradually swing round side by side and fuse completely.

(*f, g*) The single body resulting from conjugation is called a Zygospore (Gr. *zugos,* a yoke; *spora,* a seed). This zygospore bursts its case and begins to germinate.

(*h.*) The germinating Zygospore draws in its cilia, rounds itself off and divides into sixteen cells, forming a colony.

*Life History.*—Each Zoogonidium of the Pandorina-colony divides into sixteen portions— like the original—and then escapes through the gelatinous wall. This is the non-sexual mode of multiplication. The sexual reproduction consists in the production of cells

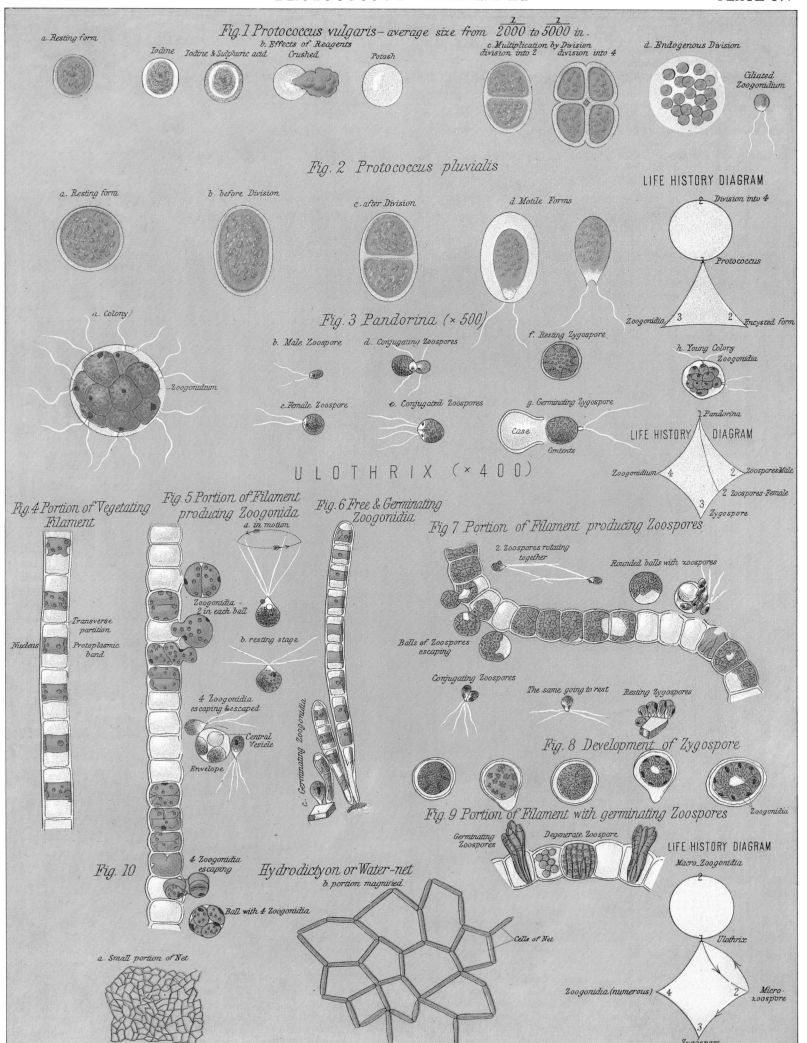

Fig. 1 Protococcus vulgaris – average size from $\frac{1}{2000}$ to $\frac{1}{5000}$ in.

a. Resting form

b. Effects of Reagents

Iodine    Iodine & Sulphuric acid    Crushed    Potash

c. Multiplication by Division
division into 2    division into 4

d. Endogenous Division

Ciliated Zoogonidium

Fig. 2 Protococcus pluvialis

a. Resting form    b. before Division    c. after Division    d. Motile Forms

LIFE HISTORY DIAGRAM
Division into 4
Protococcus
Zoogonidia   3   2   Encysted form

Fig. 3 Pandorina (× 500)

a. Colony

Zoogonidium

b. Male Zoospore    d. Conjugating Zoospores    f. Resting Zygospore    h. Young Colony Zoogonidia

c. Female Zoospore    e. Conjugated Zoospores    g. Germinating Zygospore
Case   Contents

LIFE HISTORY DIAGRAM
Pandorina
Zoogonidium   4   2   Zoospores Male
  2   Zoospores Female
3
Zygospore

ULOTHRIX (× 400)

Fig. 4 Portion of Vegetating Filament

Nucleus
Transverse partition
Protoplasmic band

Fig. 5 Portion of Filament producing Zoogonida
a. in motion
Zoogonidia 2 in each ball
b. resting stage
4 Zoogonidia escaping & escaped
Central Vesicle
Envelope

Fig. 6 Free & Germinating Zoogonidia

c. Germinating Zoogonidia

Fig 7 Portion of Filament producing Zoospores
2. Zoospores rotating together
Rounded balls with zoospores
Balls of Zoospores escaping
Conjugating Zoospores
The same going to rest
Resting Zygospores

Fig. 8 Development of Zygospore

Zoogonidia

Fig. 10
4 Zoogonidia escaping
Ball with 4 Zoogonidia

Hydrodictyon or Water-net
b. portion magnified
Cells of Net

Fig. 9 Portion of Filament with germinating Zoospores
Germinating Zoospores
Degenerate Zoospore

LIFE HISTORY DIAGRAM
Macro Zoogonidia
Ulothrix
Zoogonidia (numerous)   4   2   Micro-zoospore
3
Zygospore

a. Small portion of Net

Engraved, Printed and Published by W. & A.K. Johnston, Edinburgh & London.

which are called Zoospores, one colony forming sixteen small (male) Zoospores, another sixteen larger (female) Zoospores. Two unite to form a Zygospore, which germinates and produces a new colony.

## ULOTHRIX ZONATA.

*(after Dodel-Port.)*

Ulothrix Zonata (Gr. *oulos,* woolly or curly; *thrix,* hair), or Curly-hair Alga, may be found in fresh waters, such as brooks, drinking fountains and the like. It occurs in green tufts attached to some fixed body.

It is a simple filamentous Alga, reproducing itself non-sexually during winter and sexually during summer, but if the sexually reproductive cells fail to conjugate, they may still grow into a new plant.

### NON-SEXUAL STAGE

*Fig. 4* Portion of Filament in vegetating condition.

The cylindrical cells are placed end to end, and in each there is a green protoplasmic band about the middle containing a nucleus.

*Fig. 5* Portion of Filament exclusively producing Zoogonidia. A mother-cell may produce one, two, four, or eight zoogonidia. The inner wall of the cell passes out as an envelope surrounding them, and afterwards deliquesces to allow their escape.

*Fig. 6* The Zoogonidium is pear-shaped, with four cilia and a red eye-spot and a contractile vacuole.

(*a.*) In motion, it rotates round its long axis by means of the four cilia.

(*b.*) On coming to rest, the cilia become stiff and fall off, and the zoogonidium fixes itself, by its tapering end, to some object.

(*c.*) The zoogonidium now germinates and, by repeated division, produces a filament, as in Fig. 4.

PLATE V.
# CONFERVACEÆ, ULVACEÆ, and MYXOMYCETES.

*(Reproduction and Development principally after Oersted.)*

CONFERVACEÆ (Lat. *confervere,* to unite) are filamentous Algæ, occurring plentifully in every stagnant water, usually in great abundance round the margin. The filaments grow in length by the individual cells dividing into two. Multiplication takes place by Zoogonidia, and Conjugation has been observed in Cladophora.

*Figs. 1 and 2* Cladophora (Gr. *klados,* a branch; *phoreo,* I bear), so named from its being branched, is a very common form.
Examine a small portion in water. Filament with alternate branches forming. The top of the cell puts forth a little pocket at one side, which grows and divides like the parent filament. Secondary branches may likewise be formed, thus giving rise to bushy tufts. One or more nuclei may be present in each cell.

*Fig. 3* Treatment with Iodine, showing starch granules.
The contents are seen to be broken up into little ovoid masses called chlorophyll-corpuscles, and it is in these the starch is formed.
Yellowish—brown colour indicates protoplasm.
The darker spots are in reality dark-blue, indicating their starchy nature.
The cellulose wall is clearly differentiated from the contents.
*Fig. 4* Multiplication by Zoogonidia.

The contents of the cells break up into little masses, which round themselves off, acquire cilia, and escape by a break in the side of the wall.
*Fig. 5* Zoogonidia germinating. They lose their cilia, begin to elongate, and grow to a filament.

ULVACEÆ form flat expansions of cells, and are commonly met with on the seashore. The common green Laver (U. latissima) may be a foot square, and is so puckered and folded that it seems branched. Enteromorpha may be regarded as a tubular Ulva; and as Conjugation has been clearly observed in it, the process will be described in that connection.

*Fig. 6* Mount a small piece in water and examine.
The cells are angular from pressure, and dark spots appear in each.

*Fig. 7* Highly magnified portion. A number of the cells contain Zoogonidia. The Zoogonidia escape

by small openings on the surface, and move about in the water by means of cilia.

ENTEROMORPHA (Gr. *enteron,* intestine; *morphe,* shape), instead of being flat, like Ulva, forms a slender tube. It occurs plentifully on the seashore, attached to stones, rocks, or even seaweed, and also forms those slimy, green growths so common on the posts of piers etc. In the autumn particularly the cells give rise to innumerable actively moving Zoospores. These come together in the water, and Conjugation takes place. The result is a Zygospore, which is believed to germinate in the ensuing spring and become a new Enteromorpha.

*Fig. 8* It consists of a tapering attached end, giving off numerous small branches, then expanding till it reaches the apex, where a slender forked portion branches off a little to one side. The surface of this specimen is puckered, and here and there delicate branches are formed.
*Figs. 9 and 10* Take a small portion and examine under microscope.

The tube is seen to consist of a single layer of cells, and when spread out as in Fig.9, quite resembles the frond of Ulva.
*Fig. 11* Portion highly magnified. Some of the cells are still in the vegetative condition, others are full of Zoospores, in some the contents have escaped, and on the left side the

Zoospores are seen in the act of escaping, enveloped by the inner membrane of the cell.
*Figs. 12 and 13* Micro-zoospores free and conjugating.
Two Zoospores meet by their pointed ends, then swing round side by side, blend, lose their cilia, and become a pear-shaped Zygospore.

*Life History of Confervaceæ* and Ulvaceæ—The cells either produce Zoogondia, which grow into a new plant, or Zoospores, which conjugate, thereby forming Zygospores to reproduce the plant.

MYXOMYCETES (Gr. *muxa,* slime, *mukes* a fungus), or Slime-fungi, as their name denotes, are slimy bodies found on rotten wood, decaying leaves, etc.; and the specimen chosen—Aethalium septicum, or "flowers of tan"—occurs on spent tan. It is of a creamy, yellow colour; and in nurseries, where spent tan is used for bottom heat, it may be found in the autumn overspreading large surfaces, and, forced by the lack of heat, it has been known to make its way up the stems of plants. The limit of heat for this form is 40°C.

The Myxomycetes are peculiar in passing through an Amœboid stage, when they take in solid nutriment and feed like animals, so that in this stage of their existence at least, they resemble animals rather than plants. Their life history too is quite comparable to that of some of the lower animals, as may be seen from the Figures.

*Fig. 14* Aethalium septicum (Gr. *aithales,* splendid, from its appearance).
*(a.)* The Amœboid stage, or Myxopod of the animal series, possess a nucleus.
*(b.)* The Plasmodium stage is the large, conspicuous, yellowish mass, made up of a protoplasmic network

showing streaming of the contents as indicated by the arrows.
*(c.)* The Spore possesses a thick cell-wall, which bursts to allow the contents to escape. The rounded mass developes two cilia, which become reduced to one, and thus a body is formed like the Mastigopod of the animal series. Even this single cilium

disappears, and the Amœboid stage is reached, as at the beginning.
*Fig. 15* Sporangium of Arcyria—unopened and opened. The elasticity of the fibres composing the Capillitum (Lat. *capillus,* a hair) ultimately ruptures the case and jerks out the spores.

*Life History.*—In fixing the starting-point for the life history of the Myxomycetes I have been guided by its evident similarity to that of some of the Monera described by Haeckel, and so

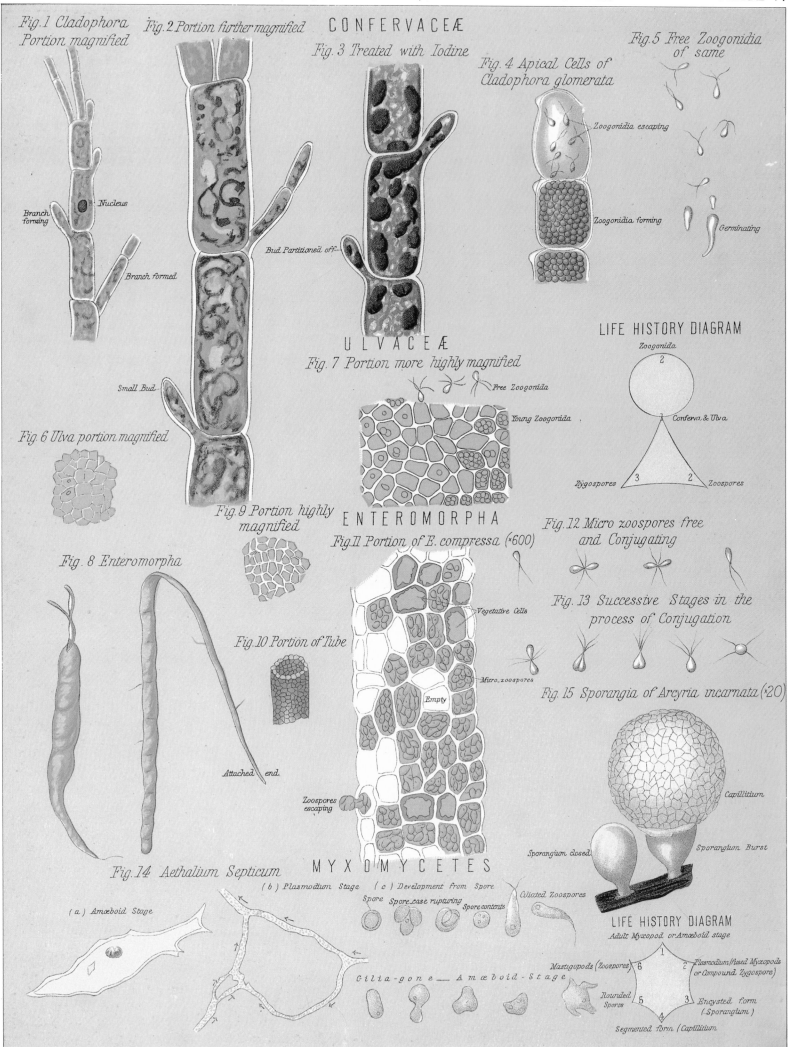

CONFERVACEÆ

Fig. 1 *Cladophora Portion magnified*

Fig. 2 *Portion further magnified*

Fig. 3 *Treated with Iodine*

Fig. 4 *Apical Cells of Cladophora glomerata*

Fig. 5 *Free Zoogonidia of same*

Branch forming — Nucleus — Branch formed — Small Bud — Bud Partitioned off — Zoogonidia escaping — Zoogonidia forming — Germinating

ULVACEÆ

Fig. 7 *Portion more highly magnified*

Fig. 6 *Ulva portion magnified*

Free Zoogonida — Young Zoogonida

ENTEROMORPHA

Fig. 9 *Portion highly magnified*

Fig. 8 *Enteromorpha*

Fig. 10 *Portion of Tube*

Fig. 11 *Portion of E. compressa* (×600)

Attached end — Vegetative Cells — Micro zoospores — Empty — Zoospores escaping

LIFE HISTORY DIAGRAM

Zoogonida — 2 — Conferva & Ulva — Zygospores — 3 — 2 — Zoospores

Fig. 12 *Micro zoospores free and Conjugating*

Fig. 13 *Successive Stages in the process of Conjugation*

Fig. 15 *Sporangia of Arcyria incarnata* (×20)

Capillitium — Sporangium closed — Sporangium Burst

MYXOMYCETES

Fig. 14 *Aethalium Septicum*

(a) *Amœboid Stage* — (b) *Plasmodium Stage* — (c) *Development from Spore*

Spore — Spore-case rupturing — Spore contents — Ciliated Zoospores

Cilia-gone — Amœboid-Stage

LIFE HISTORY DIAGRAM

Adult Myxopod or Amœboid stage — 1 — Plasmodium (fused Myxopods or Compound Zygospore) 2 — Mastigopods (Zoospores) 6 — Encysted form (Sporangium) 3 — Rounded Spores 5 — Segmented form (Capillitium) 4

Engraved, Printed and Published by W. & A.K. Johnston, Edinburgh.

start with the Amœboid form as the first stage in the cycle. If the phases through which it passes are compared with those of Protomyxa—an undoubted animal found in the sea by Haeckel—it will be found that the agreement is striking.

The first, or Amœboid stage, has all the characters of an amœba, possessing a nucleus, throwing out processes in different directions, moving about, and taking in solid particles for food.

The second, or Plasmodium stage, consists of a number of amœboid masses run together to form one large spreading mass capable of a creeping motion, as already observed, along with internal motion of the contents. The nuclei of each originally independent mass remain distinct, so that there is coalescence of cells but not conjugation.

The third, or Encysted stage, is represented by the Sporangium. The irregularly-shaped Plasmodium assumes a more definite shape as its power of throwing out processes becomes weakened, and usually forms a rounded mass of protoplasm   invested by a cellulose wall.

The fourth, or Segmented stage, is produced by the internal protoplasm, differentiating in such a way as to form a network of fibres, and the protoplasm still remaining in the meshes becomes the Spores. The hair-like structure, in the meshes of which the Spores are developed, is known as the Capillitium.

The fifth stage, or Rounded Spores. The contents of the liberated Spores escape and become—

The sixth stage, or Zoospores, which have two cilia, then one, and finally pass into the Amœboid form with which we started.

It will be evident from the above description that the Myxomycetes cannot retain their position among the conjugating forms of Fungi ; and even when their animal nature is considered they do not fall into the lowest strata either of Plant or Animal society.

PLATE VI.

# SPIROGYRA, DESMIDS, and DIATOMS.

*(Spirogyra chiefly after Sachs; Desmid and Diatom after Oersted.)*

SPIROGYRA (Gr. *guros,* a ring) is readily recognised under the microscope from the spiral bands of green-coloured protoplasm. It floats in bright green masses near the surface of clear, fresh waters, such as ponds, and slips through the fingers on attempting to handle it.

The bands of coloured protoplasm are variable in their number and arrangement. They contain numerous starch-granules and oil globules, and a nucleus is present in each cell. This condensed portion of the protoplasm is surrounded by a layer of protoplasm, which sends delicate threads towards the cell-wall, giving the nucleus a star-like appearance. There is also a layer of protoplasm lining the cell-wall, to which these threads are attached, and this lining is made very evident by the application of iodine, which causes the protoplasm to contract and withdraw itself from the wall. The protoplasm is broken up into shreds and bands, because, being unable to fill the cell, the cavities are filled with cell-sap, and these, by spreading and increasing, finally leave the protoplasm in this scattered form. Protoplasm thus on the stretch, as it were, displays much of its intimate nature, which is concealed in the more uniform condition.

Multiplication of the cells takes place by Division, and Reproduction by Conjugation.

*Fig. 1* Either take a small portion of the water in which odd pieces are floating, or a minute portion of the green mass, and examine under highest power.

Long filaments made up of cells, with distinct walls and green spiral bands, in which numerous granules are visible.

*Diagram*—Showing arrangement of bands.

Careful focussing is necessary to make out the exact continuity of the bands, and this may be made out better after treatment with reagents than in natural specimens.

In this particular species the bands are arranged in two spirals, which intersect each other. In S. longata (Fig. 4) there is but a single spiral band.

*Fig 2* Stain with Iodine.

Iodine makes the nucleus prominent,

turns the starch-granules blue, and causes the layer of protoplasm lining the cell-wall to contract about the spiral bands. This layer of protoplasm has received the name of "primordial utricle," but it is simply a portion of the protoplasm which lines the cell-wall.

*Fig. 3* As division takes place during night, in order to get cells in the act of division place them in alcohol shortly after mid-night and examine with highest power.

The cellulose is seen to be extending inwards on each side.

*Fig. 4a* Cell in the living state, with single nucleus and regularly-arranged bands.

*b* Protoplasm contracted by the alcohol. Infolding of the protoplasm lining the wall, and cellulose formed in the notch.

Two nuclei formed during division,

one for each new cell.

*c* Infolding further advanced, which would ultimately form a complete partition across.

*Figs. 5 and 6* Conjugation.

Two filaments lay themselves alongside each other, and adjoining cells of each filament throw out pockets simultaneously towards each other, which eventually meet and form a connecting *tube* between the two cells. The contents of one cell pass over and fuse with that of the other, the nuclei also coalescing, thus producing a Zygospore, as in Fig. 6.

*Fig. 7* Germination.

The outer wall of the Zygospore ruptures, and the innermost layer protrudes as a filament, gradually growing and forming transverse partitions until a proper filament is produced.

DESMIDS (Gr. *desmos,* a band) are beautiful, minute, green plants, found in fresh water, and consisting usually of a single cell. The cells are generally divided into two symmetrical halves, and the coloured protoplasm is arranged in bands.

Multiplication by Division is shown in next Plate. Sexual reproduction by Conjugation is shown here.

*Fig. 8* Different views of Cosmarium, showing the two halves and the coloured bands.

*Fig. 9* Two cells approach one another, the narrow waist ruptures, and the

contents of each fuse.

*Fig. 10* A single rounded mass is formed, with the empty halves of each Desmid still adhering to it.

*Fig. 11* The Zygospore secretes a cellulose wall, which grows out into

beautiful spines.

*Fig. 12* The Zygospore escapes from its case and begins to germinate.

*Fig. 13* Zygospore divides into two new Desmids, which lie across each other.

DIATOMS (Gr. *dia,* through; *temno,* I cut) are so named from the common genus Diatoma, in which the cell-walls, or Frustules (Lat. *frustum,* a fragment), remain connected in a zigzag fashion after each division, looking like a continuous structure cut up into a number of similar fragments. Various forms are sure to be met with while examining fresh-water Algæ, Euglena, and the like.

They are unicellular like the Desmids, but are yellowish in colour, have not the characteristic median constriction, and their cell-walls are silicious, exhibiting on their surface those beautiful markings which are a never-ending source of delight and interest to the microscopist. It is owing to this indestructible character of the cell-wall that Diatoms form geological deposits, and their beautiful structure has been preserved as finely as those living at the present day. The Diatom muds, of a pale straw colour, beneath peat-mosses, have acquired great importance recently from being used in the manufacture of dynamite, which is a combination of the silicious material with nitro-glycerine.

They exhibit slow movement from place to place, and exposed to light in considerable numbers they evolve oxygen.

28

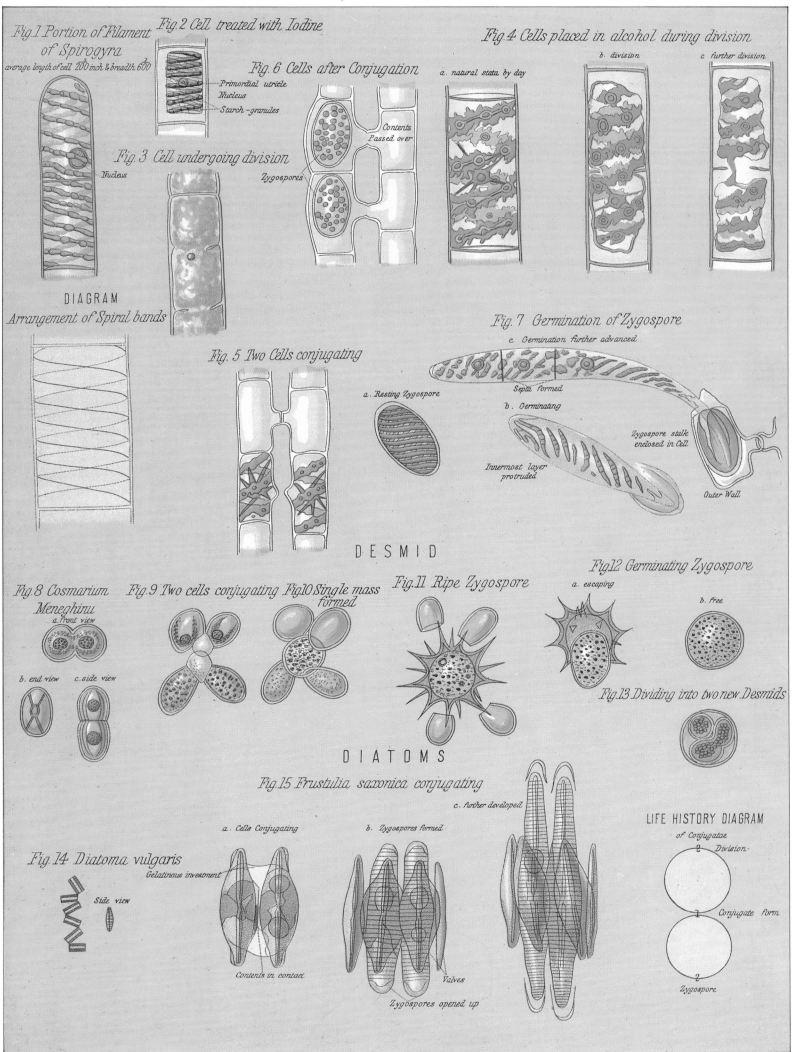

Fig.1 Portion of Filament of Spirogyra
average length of cell 200 inch & breadth 600
Nucleus

Fig.2 Cell treated with Iodine
Primordial utricle
Nucleus
Starch-granules

Fig.3 Cell undergoing division
Nucleus

DIAGRAM
Arrangement of Spiral bands

Fig. 6 Cells after Conjugation
Contents Passed over
Zygospores

Fig.4 Cells placed in alcohol during division
a. natural state by day
b. division
c. further division

Fig. 5 Two Cells conjugating

Fig. 7 Germination of Zygospore
c. Germination further advanced
a. Resting Zygospore
b. Germinating
Septa formed
Zygospore stalk enclosed in Cell
Innermost layer protruded
Outer Wall

DESMID

Fig.8 Cosmarium Meneghinu
a. front view
b. end view
c. side view

Fig.9 Two cells conjugating

Fig.10 Single mass formed

Fig.11 Ripe Zygospore

Fig.12 Germinating Zygospore
a. escaping
b. free

Fig.13 Dividing into two new Desmids

DIATOMS

Fig.15 Frustulia saxonica conjugating
c. further developed.
a. Cells Conjugating
Gelatinous investment
b. Zygospores formed
Valves
Contents in contact.
Zygospores opened up

Fig.14 Diatoma vulgaris
Side view

LIFE HISTORY DIAGRAM
of Conjugatae
2 Division
1 Conjugate Form
2 Zygospore

Engraved, Printed and Published by W. & A.K. Johnston, Edinburgh

SPIROGYRA, etc.—*continued.*

Multiplication takes place by Division, Reproduction by Conjugation.

*Fig. 14* Diatoma, a very common form. The cells formed by successive divisions remain slightly attached.
*Fig. 15* Conjugation of Frustulia saxonica.

(*a.*) Two Diatoms beside each other surround themselves with a gelatinous mass, the valves then fall apart like an opened book, and the contents of each come together, but do not mix.

(*b.*) Next, the two contents clothe themselves with a delicate membrane, elongate, and form two Zygospores.
(*c.*) Each Zygospore now forms two valves, and becomes fully formed.

30

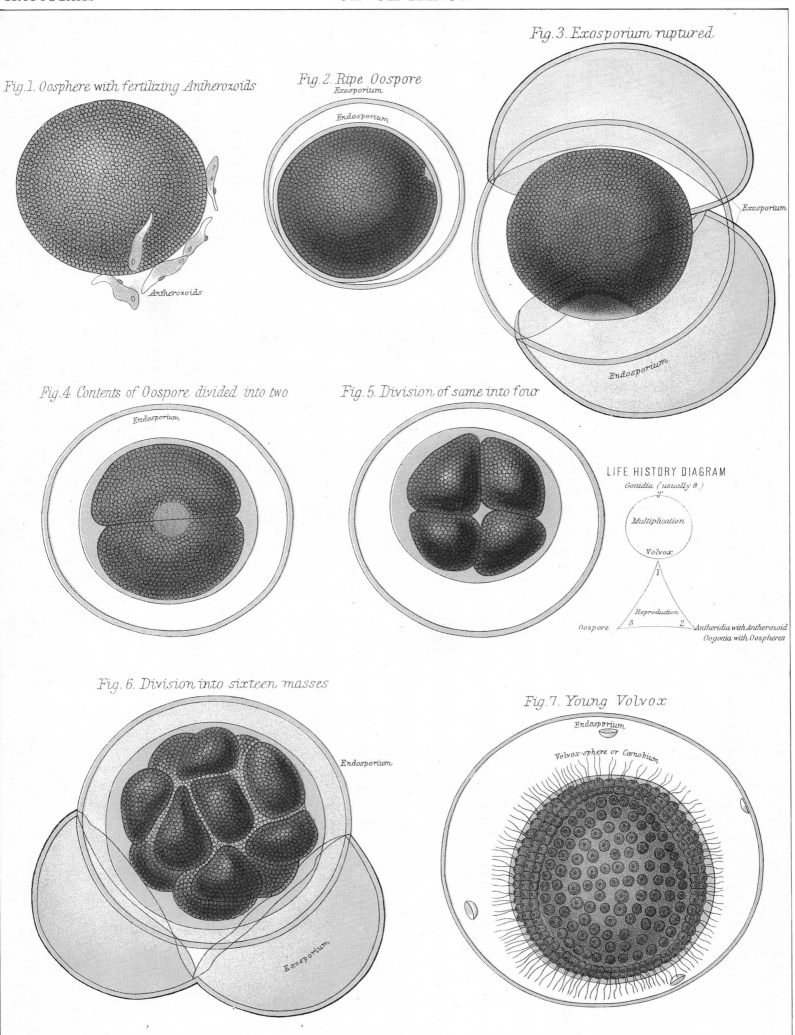

Fig. 1. Oosphere with fertilizing Antherozoids

Antheroxoids

Fig. 2. Ripe Oospore

Exosporium

Endosporium

Fig. 3. Exosporium ruptured

Exosporium

Endosporium

Fig. 4. Contents of Oospore divided into two

Endosporium

Fig. 5. Division of same into four

Fig. 6. Division into sixteen masses

Endosporium

Exosporium

Fig. 7. Young Volvox

Endosporium

Volvox-sphere or Cœnobium

LIFE HISTORY DIAGRAM

Gonidia (usually 8)

Multiplication

Volvox

Reproduction

Oospore     Antheridia with Antherozoid
Oogonia with Oospheres

Engraved, Printed and Published by W. & A.K. Johnston, Edinburgh & London.

PLATE XI.

# VAUCHERIA and ŒDOGONIUM.

## VAUCHERIA.

Vaucheria, named in honour of the Swiss botanist Vaucher, occurs usually on damp soils as a green film, but may readily be obtained from the surface earth of flower-pots kept in green-houses. It is a long filamentous green Alga, consisting of a single tubular cell which branches, and also forms root-like structures.

*Fig. 1* Take a small portion of the green film, tease it out in a drop of water, and examine under microscope. Filament showing the granular protoplasm lining interior of tube.

### MULTIPLICATION

*Fig. 2* End of branches forming Zoogonidia.
These are formed during night, by the protoplasm, towards the end of a tube, collecting itself into an oval mass and becoming separate from the rest by a partition. The end of the tube gives way allowing this oval mass to escape into the surrounding moisture, where it revolves and progresses by means of delicate cilia with which the whole surface is covered. The cilia, however, soon disappear, and the motionless mass then sinks to the bottom.

*Fig. 3a, b, c* Germinating Zoogonidium—It gives rise to filaments at two or even three points, which branch and grow to the size of the parent. Delicate transparent branches are also formed (as in *c*) which serve to fix the plant to solid bodies, and thus partly serve the purpose of rootlets.

### REPRODUCTION

*Figs. 4 and 5* Male and Female Organs—Antheridia and Oogonia. Both organs arise as branches, sometimes as in Fig. 4, or as in Fig. 5, where a branch ends in a hooked Antheridium, with an Oogonium on each side below it.
The contents of the Antheridium break up into minute particles of protoplasm, each furnished with two cilia and motile—called Antherozoids. The Oogonium forms a single body in its interior-the Oosphere which is a portion of the protoplasm marked off from the rest by a partition. It is relatively large and motionless, and the antherozoids find access to it through a rupture in the cell-wall, thus converting it into an Oospore.

*Fig. 6* Germinating Oospore.
The Oospore is surrounded by a three-layered membrane and, after resting for a few months, the contents protrude to form a branching tube.

*Life History.*—Vaucheria either multiplies by Zoogonidia, or reproduces itself by means of Antherozoids and Oospheres. The naked protoplasm of the Antherozoids blends with the naked protoplasm of the Oosphere, and the result is a body capable of germination—an Oosphere. This surrounds itself with a membrane, becomes detached along with the Oogonium, and is finally set free by the dissolution of the Oogonium. After a period of rest it germinates and gives rise to the original branched structure.

## ŒDOGONIUM

### (*After Juranyi.*)

Œdogonium (Gr. *oideo,* to swell; *gone,* seed) derives its name from the fact that the joints of the filament swell out to form the female organs. It may be looked for in waters where Conferva and such organisms are found, and occurs as patches of green filaments, composed of cells attached end to end.

*Fig. 7* Young Filament, consisting of a row of cells.
The green-coloured protoplasm is arranged in stars and stripes, and each cell has a distinct nucleus.

### MULTIPLICATION

*Fig. 8* Zoogonidia produced in the cells.
The protoplasmic contents of each cell form a single rounded mass—the Zoogonidium, which escapes by a fissure in the wall, and revolves and progresses by means of the band of cilia.
*Fig. 9* Germination of Zoogonidium.
The zoogonidium loses its cilia and settles down, producing from the colourless ciliated end a root-like structure for fixing the plant, while the opposite end divides and forms a row of cells.

### REPRODUCTION

*Fig. 10* Male Filament.
The contents of certain cells become orange-yellow and produce the Antherozoids, which resemble the Zoogonidia in form and motion, differing mainly in the colour. In some cases, however, zoogonidia are formed in the cells, which become rudimentary plants, and the sole object of these *Dwarf-males,* as they are called, is to produce Antherozoids. They attach themselves to the Oogonium, as in Fig. I2, and the upper portion separates like a lid to allow the antherozoids to escape.
*Figs. 11 and 12* Female Filaments.
The joints here and there are swollen, forming the Oogonia, which contain the Oospheres. The ripe Oosphere consists of a coloured and a small colourless portion, which protrudes through a small opening.

*Fig. 13* Process of Fertilisation.
An Antherozoid blends with an Oosphere, and the result is an Oospore.
*Fig. 14* Ripe Oospore.
It becomes surrounded with a membrane, and assumes an orange-red colour. The swelling of the Oospore finally ruptures the Oogonium, and the oospore escapes as a naked mass of protoplasm.
*Figs 15, 16, and 17* Germinating Oospores. The germinating Oospore does not grow in the usual way, but surrounds itself with a new membrane, and the contents divide into four portions generally. The Zoospores thus formed are set free by the dissolution of the membrane, and produce a young plant, as in Fig. 17.

*Life History.*—Œdogonium multiplies by Zoogonidia, or is reproduced by Antherozoids and Oospheres. An Antherozoid produced either directly from the joint of a filament or through the intermediate agency of Dwarf-males, blends with the Oosphere and produces an orange-red Oosphere. This Oosphere does not directly produce the Plant, but divides into usually four Zoospores, like the zoogonidia, except in the matter of colour, and each germinates and grows into a filament, as in Fig. 17.

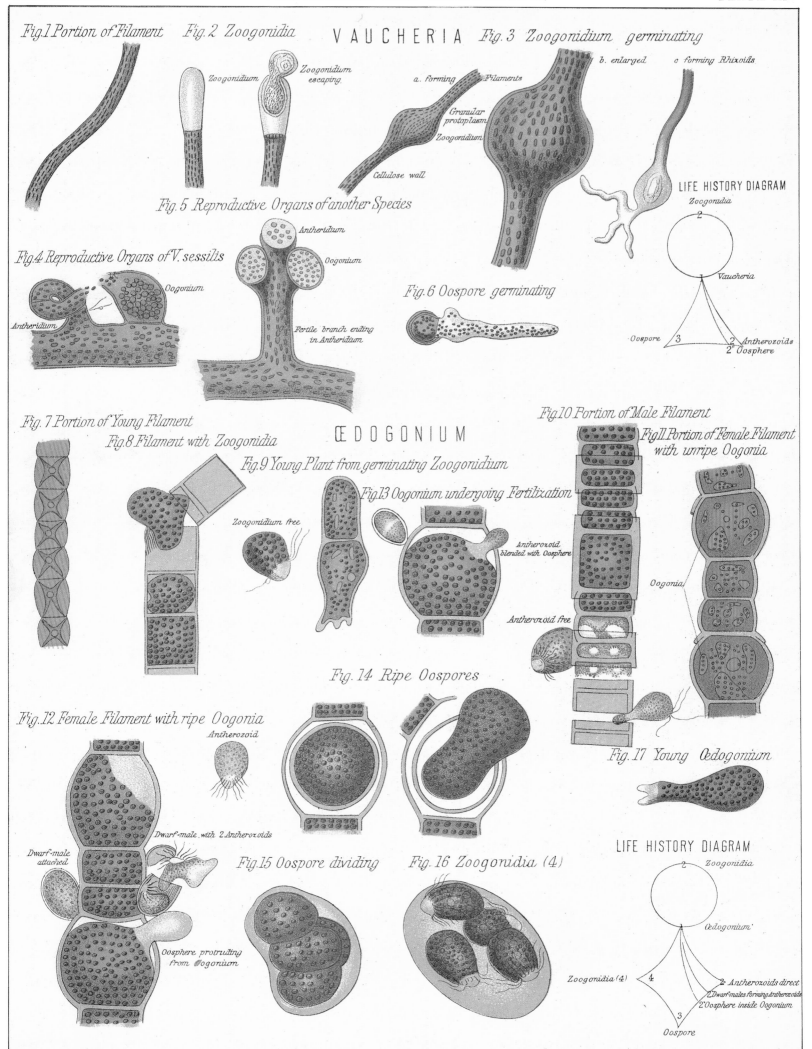

Fig.1 Portion of Filament    Fig.2 Zoogonidia    VAUCHERIA    Fig.3 Zoogonidium germinating

Zoogonidium

Zoogonidium escaping.

a. forming   Filaments    b. enlarged    c forming Rhizoids

Granular protoplasm

Zoogonidium

Cellulose wall

LIFE HISTORY DIAGRAM

Zoogonidia

Vaucheria

Oospore    Antherozoids   Oosphere

Fig. 5 Reproductive Organs of another Species

Antheridium

Oogonium

Fig.4 Reproductive Organs of V. sessilis

Oogonium

Antheridium

Fertile branch ending in Antheridium

Fig. 6 Oospore germinating

Fig. 7 Portion of Young Filament

Fig.8 Filament with Zoogonidia

ŒDOGONIUM

Fig.10 Portion of Male Filament

Fig.11 Portion of Female Filament with unripe Oogonia

Fig.9 Young Plant from germinating Zoogonidium

Fig.13 Oogonium undergoing Fertilization

Zoogonidium free

Antherozoid blended with Oosphere

Antherozoid free

Oogonia

Fig.14 Ripe Oospores

Fig.17 Young Œdogonium

Fig.12 Female Filament with ripe Oogonia

Antherozoid

Dwarf-male with 2 Antherozoids

Dwarf-male attached

Fig.15 Oospore dividing    Fig.16 Zoogonidia (4)

LIFE HISTORY DIAGRAM

Zoogonidia

Œdogonium

Oosphere protruding from Oogonium

Zoogonidia (4)

Antherozoids direct

Dwarf-males forming Antherozoids

Oosphere inside Oogonium

Oospore

Engraved, Printed and Published by W. & A.K. Johnston, Edinburgh & London.

PLATE XII.

# POTATO-DISEASE FUNGUS (*Phytophthora infestans*).

*(Principally after De Bary.)*

The Potato-disease Fungus was formerly known as *Peronospora*, but the fuller investigation of its history has caused it to be placed in the genus *Phytopthora*. Although its life-history has been traced to a certain extent, yet, as in the case of Rust of Wheat and other parasitic fungi, a satisfactory mode of dealing with the disease has not yet been found.

It is but fair to add that some consider this fungus-growth as a consequence and not as a cause of the disease. They maintain that a fungus cannot establish itself upon a living plant, until that plant has become enfeebled; and further, that before any appearance of the disease in the potato could be detected by the eye or microscope, it was possible to reveal it by a simple chemical test. This was done by using a minute borer and taking a thread of the potato bored out and placing it in a flask with milk in a warm closet. If the milk curdled in a very short time, the potato was found to be diseased; and if healthy, no curdling took place. The diseased potato soon showed signs of decay and of premature germination, and so the actual disease is supposed to be antecedent to the appearance of the fungus.

*Fig. 1* Diseased Leaf of Potato. The infected parts of the leaf turn black.

*Figs. 2 and 3* Hypha bearing Stylo-gonidia. The filament bores its way through the tissues of the plant, absorbs and appropriates their nutriment, and gradually traverses the whole plant.

Eventually it puts forth hyphæ through the stomata of the leaf, which branch and bear capsules styled *Stylo-gonidia*.

*Figs. 4, 5, and 6* The contents of the Stylo-gonidium break up into separate portions (usually six), which escape by rupturing the wall.

*Fig. 7* Each Zoogonidium possess a pair of cilia, and through the medium of rain or dew may find their way from one plant to another and thus infect a whole field.

*Fig. 8* Zoogonidium germinating. The inner membrane protrudes as a filament, penetrating the epidermis, and begins to ramify through the underlying tissue.

*Life History.* — The fungus traversing the potato-plant bears aerial hyphae with Stylo-gonidia, the contents of which break up into Zoogonidia. These motile Zoogonidia, on reaching the epidermis of a potato-plant, germinate to form a unicellular filament which branches among the tissues and becomes like the parent-form. This is the non-sexual mode of multiplication, but a sexual process has not yet been observed.

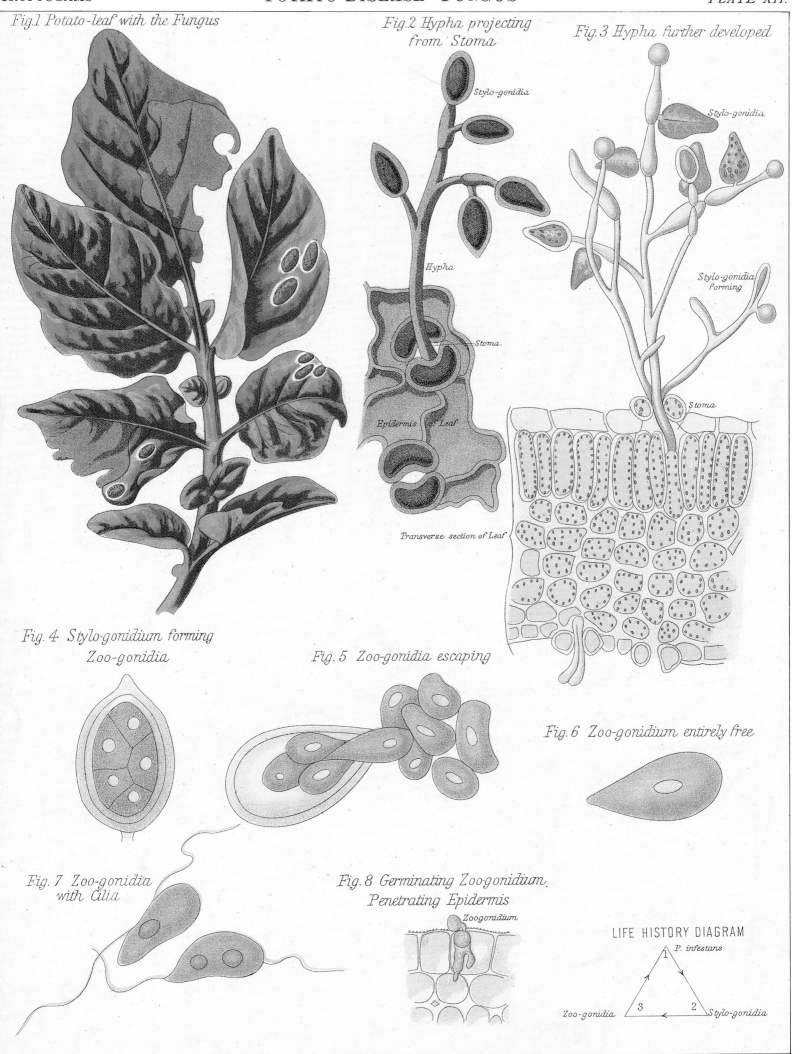

Fig.1 Potato-leaf with the Fungus

Fig.2 Hypha projecting from Stoma

*Stylo-gonidia*

*Hypha*

*Stoma.*

*Epidermis of Leaf*

*Transverse section of Leaf*

Fig.3 Hypha further developed

*Stylo-gonidia*

*Stylo-gonidia forming*

*Stoma*

Fig. 4 Stylo-gonidium forming Zoo-gonidia

Fig. 5 Zoo-gonidia escaping

Fig. 6 Zoo-gonidium entirely free

Fig. 7 Zoo-gonidia with Cilia

Fig. 8 Germinating Zoo-gonidium Penetrating Epidermis

*Zoogonidium*

LIFE HISTORY DIAGRAM

*P. infestans*

1

3     2

*Zoo-gonidia*     *Stylo-gonidia*

Engraved, Printed and Published by W. & A.K. Johnston, Edinburgh.

PLATE XIII.

# COMMON BLADDER WRACK (*Fucus vesiculosus*) and TANGLE (*Laminaria digitata*).

Fucus (G. *phukos*, sea-weed) and Laminaria (Lat. *lamina*, a thin plate) may be taken as representatives of the brown-coloured sea-weeds. They are common objects of the shore wherever rocks abound.

In *Fucus*, the flat expansion or Thallus is dichotomously branched, and attached to the rocks by suckers, so that there is a superficial resemblance to stem, roots, and leaves. But it is only superficial, since the whole plant is bathed with sea-water from which, and not from the soil or air, every part withdraws its appropriate nourishment. The root-like portion consists of delicate hair-like branches with thin cell-walls. It acts like a boy's sucker; it can be pressed very close to the rock, and the pressure of the water, just like the air in the previous case, keeps the two together.

The stem-like narrow portion, as well as the more expanded upper portion, is slimy all over, and this is due to the cell-walls of the outer cells becoming mucilaginous.

The air-bladders serving the purpose of floats contain various gases.

The reproductive organs are borne by the swollen ends of branches and developed in little cavities known as Conceptacles. These are seen by the naked eye as little elevations with openings, and have been formed by a pushing-in or indentation of the exterior. Each dimple or Conceptacle contains Antheridia with Antherozoids or male organs, and Oogonia with Oospheres or female organs.

The most common species are *F. vesiculosis* (Lat. *vesicula*, a little bladder) with a midrib running along each part of the thallus, and air-bladders arranged in a double row; *F. nodosus*, with air-bladders arranged singly and no midrib; and *F. serratus* (Lat. *serra*, a saw) destitute of air-bladders and margins toothed.

*Laminaria digitata* (Lat. *digitus*, the finger) is so named because the expanded portion is split up like the fingers of the hand. It has a root-like portion consisting of numerous branching stalks expanded at their attached end; a stem-like portion which is perennial, and increases in thickness by concentric layers added year after year; and the split-up leaf-like portion which is renewed every year.

Multiplication takes place by Zoogonidia developed from the expanded portion. Sexual reproduction is as yet unknown.

*Fig. 1* Portion of plant, natural size. Thallus branching in a forked manner or dichotomously, with a well-marked midrib.
Air-bladders occurring in a double series.
Fertile branches swollen and studded over with yellow papillæ.
*Fig. 2* Make a transverse section of a fertile branch, so as to get one of these little papillae in section which are called Conceptacles. There is a confused mass of hairs, amongst which may be seen the male and female organs. The close-set cells of the exterior are continued right round the Conceptacle, thus suggesting an infolding of the exterior and not an interior cavity afterwards opening externally.
Antheridia, branching hairs.

Oogonia, swollen hairs.
*Figs. 3 and 4* Take some of the yellow colouring matter from Conceptacle and mix with salt-water to see Antheridial hairs and Oogonia clearly, Antheridial hairs repeatedly branched, the ends of the branches swollen and filled with yellow granular matter. When ripe the contents of these cells consist of Antherozoids each provided with two cilia whereby they move rapidly about in the water.
Oogonia are globular bodies, derived from a single cell and producing eight Oospheres. The protoplasm of the surrounding hairs and stalk is broken up into threads, because of the numerous vacuoles formed, owing to the cells getting too large for their contents, as in Spirogyra.
*Fig. 5* Oogonium discharging its

contents.
The wall of the Oogonium consists of two layers—an outer, inelastic, which splits, and an inner, extensible, which stretches a deal before giving way. The Oospheres are discharged into the conceptacle, then into the surrounding water.
*Fig. 6* The liberated Oospheres meet with Antherozoids which surround them, blend with them, and convert them into Oospores, ready to germinate.
*Fig. 7* Germination of an Oospore. It first becomes pear-shaped, then divides into two, and the tapering end soon develops organs of attachment. The upper end divides further and further in all the dimensions of space until the adult form is attained.

*Life History*.—Fucus reproduces itself sexually by Antheridia and Oogonia, either produced together or on separate plants. The Antherozoids or the Antheridia fertilise the Oospheres of the Oogonia after being set free, and each Oospore thus produced may develop a new plant.

## HISTOLOGY.

*Fig. 8* Make a transverse section of the narrow stem-like portion, and examine in alcohol or glycerine under low power.
Cells close-set towards exterior, but arranged loosely in interior.
*Fig. 9* Stain transverse section with magenta, and examine under high power.
Cells are round, oval, or elongated,

and cell-walls very gelatinous.
*Fig. 10* Cut across Tangle and examine—*first*, with naked eye; *second*, a transverse section under low power.
(*a.*) Outer yellowish-brown portion, and inner colourless portion.
(*b.*) Outer coloured portion, small and close-set cells. In old specimens there is a ring of oval slime-cavities pretty near one another. Inner almost

colourless portion of larger cells.
*Fig. 11* Make a longitudinal section, and examine interior cells as in Fucus. The elongated cells are bounded by a firm inner membrane, and between this membrane, of two adjoining cells, there is a gelatinous intercellular substance often arranged in layers. Short Pits occur here and there in the membrane.

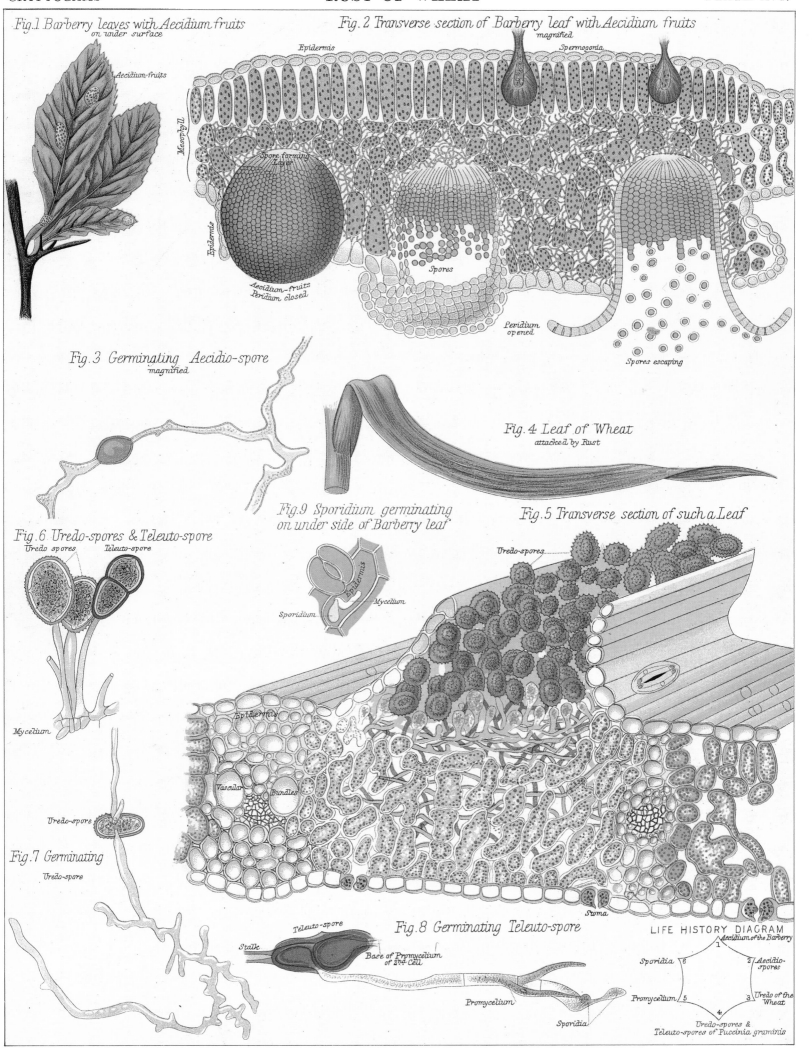

Fig.1 Barberry leaves with Aecidium fruits
on under surface

Aecidium-fruits

Fig.2 Transverse section of Barberry leaf with Aecidium fruits
magnified

Epidermis

Spermogonia

Mesophyll

Spore forming Layer

Epidermis

Spores

Aecidium-fruits
Peridium closed

Peridium opened

Spores escaping

Fig.3 Germinating Aecidio-spore
magnified

Fig.4 Leaf of Wheat
attacked by Rust

Fig.9 Sporidium germinating
on under side of Barberry leaf

Fig.5 Transverse section of such a Leaf

Uredo-spores

Epidermis

Sporidium   Mycelium

Fig.6 Uredo-spores & Teleuto-spore

Uredo spores   Teleuto-spore

Mycelium

Epidermis

Vascular   Bundles

Fig.7 Germinating

Uredo-spore

Uredo-spore

Stoma

Fig.8 Germinating Teleuto-spore

Teleuto-spore

Stalk

Base of Promycelium
of 2nd Cell

Promycelium

Sporidia

LIFE HISTORY DIAGRAM

Aecidium of the Barberry

1

Sporidia   6

2   Aecidio-spores

Promycelium   5

3   Uredo of the Wheat

4

Uredo-spores &
Teleuto-spores of Puccinia graminis

Engraved, Printed and Published by W. & A.K. Johnston, Edinburgh

PLATE XVII.

# COMMON MUSHROOM (*Agaricus campestris*) and RED SEA-WEED (*Polysiphonia*).

## MUSHROOM.

The Pezizae are distinguished by producing their spores in the *interior* of cells called Asci, and the Mushroom produces its spores on the *exterior* of enlarged cells called Basidia, hence the name applied to the group—*Basidiomycetes*. The common Mushroom may be found towards the end of summer in open pastures, but it can be raised from spawn at any season of the year. Mushroom spawn simply consists of the mycelium mixed up with decaying organic matter, and under proper treatment, as to moisture and temperature, mushrooms may be produced.

Although the mushroom belongs to the most highly organised group of *Fungi,* just as the Red Sea-weed belongs to the highest group of *Algae,* yet no sexual stage has yet been discovered.

*Fig. 1* Mushroom, full grown.
The mycelium consists of interlacing threads spread out in the mould, and what is called the Mushroom is really the Spore-fruit arising from this mycelium.
Spore-fruit composed of—Stalk with a remnant surrounding it near the top, of what once extended to the margin of the Cap.
Cap spread out like an umbrella, and bearing on its under surface the radiating plate-like Gills.
*Fig. 2* Young Mushroom, entire and in section.
The cap and stalk are already roughly indicated.
The section shows the commencement of the gill-chamber, which is really a hollow ring in which the gills are formed.
*Fig. 3* Mushroom more advanced—in section.

Velum (Lat. *a veil*), forming a floor to the gill-chamber from the roof of which the gills are developed.
*Fig. 4* Remove a gill, embed it in paraffin, and make a section of it. The centre is occupied by mycelial filaments closely packed and adhering side by side, and towards each surface this tissue becomes denser on the outside, giving rise to the Basidia.
*Fig. 5* Section under high power. Towards the surface the cells get rounded and the superficial layer of cells is enlarged to form Basidia. The Basidium has four slender processes (two only shown), at the end of which the spores are developed and easily detached.
*Fig. 6* Germination of Spore of Coprinus.—The spores may be readily obtained by laying the Spore-fruit upon a sheet of paper, then by placing over the spores a glass slide

moistened by the breath, they may be lifted up and examined.
The spore placed in a drop of an appropriate fluid on a slide begins to germinate in a few hours by putting forth a delicate filament. This grows, becomes divided by transverse partitions and branches, thus forming a mycelium. In the course of from nine to twelve days the Spore-fruit arises directly from the older mycelial filaments.
*Fig. 7* In some cases however, a Sclerotium is formed first.—This consists originally of an aerial branch, which divides and branches on all sides till it forms a small ball of closely packed and interosculating filaments. One of the surface-cells grows out and becomes the young spore-fruit, which, in this instance, is entirely invested by the velum.

*Life History.*—It is very tempting to suppose that the Spore-fruit is the result of a sexual process, but as experiments specially directed to that point have failed to show any trace of it, it is now generally believed that in the whole of the Basidio-mycetes the Spore-fruit arises directly from the mycelium or indirectly from a Sclerotium.

The stages through which they pass would be briefly as follows:—the Mycelium (or Spawn) produces a Spore-fruit directly, which bears the numerous spores from which the mycelium is again produced, and so on; or, in some cases, the Spore-fruit is preceded by a Sclerotium.

## RED SEA-WEED.

Polysiphonia (Gr. *polus,* many; *siphon,* a tube) is one of the Red Sea-weeds—plants usually of a graceful form and beautiful colour, so that they attract attention. This form is found about low-water mark, attached to rocks, the stalks of the Tangle, etc., and although so finely divided, it may be removed from the water without collapsing. These divisions might be regarded as of the nature of leaves, just as in the next form considered (Chara). There are three distinct forms of this plant, all agreeing in general appearance, but differing in their reproductive habit—the Non-sexual, the Male and the Female; and it is the first of these which will be considered now.

*Fig. 8* Plant much divided.
*Fig. 9* Plocamium is one of the feathery red sea-weeds, and when simply spread out in water under the microscope, it shows clearly the single growing cell—cells a little further back dividing longitudinally to produce breadth, and a single cell growing laterally and dividing to form one of the numerous branches. The cell-walls

are gelatinous.
*Fig. 10* Portion of Non-sexual plant showing Tetragonidia.
They appear as little round balls, but under a high power division is seen. The four gonidia do not lie in one plane, but are arranged like a tetrahedron; hence, either one or three divisions may be seen.

The gonidia escape by a parting between the peripheral cells.
*Fig. 11* Germination. The Gonidium elongates, divides transversely, one of the divisions serving for attachment, the other growing and dividing longitudinally and transversely, and branching, till it becomes a parent plant.

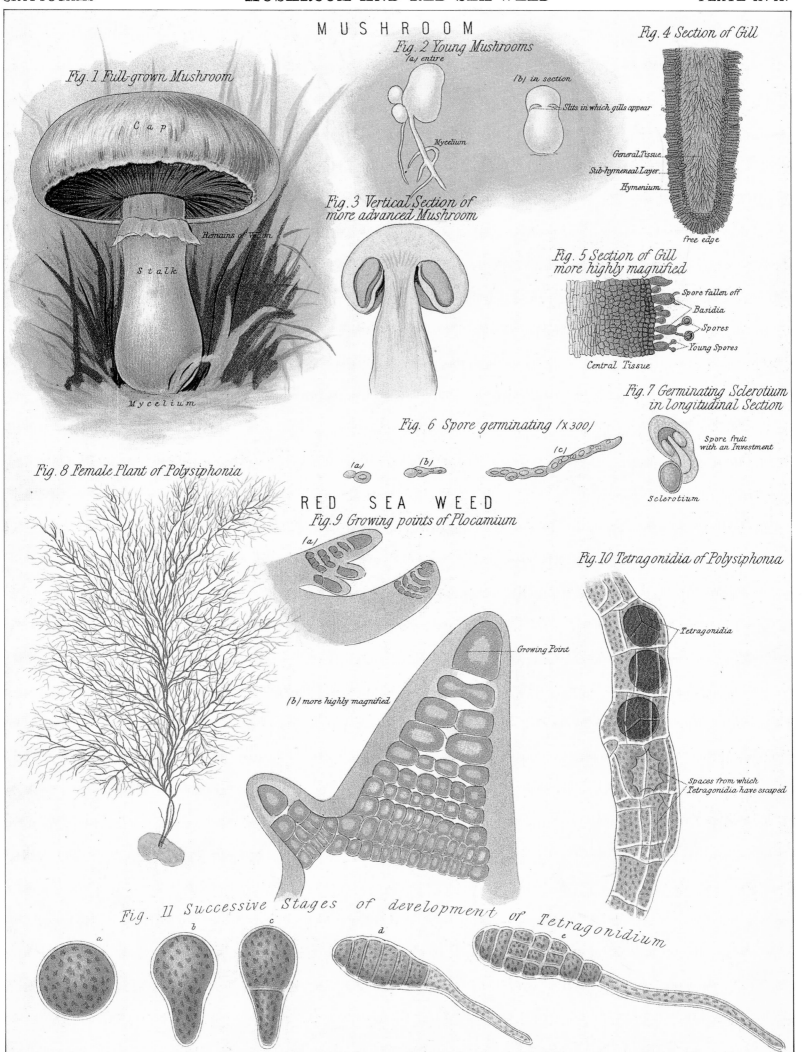

MUSHROOM

*Fig. 2 Young Mushrooms*
*(a) entire*
*(b) in section*
Slits in which gills appear
*Mycelium*

*Fig. 4 Section of Gill*
General Tissue
Sub-hymeneal Layer
Hymenium
free edge

*Fig. 1 Full-grown Mushroom*
Cap
Remains of Veil
Stalk
Mycelium

*Fig. 3 Vertical Section of more advanced Mushroom*

*Fig. 5 Section of Gill more highly magnified*
Spore fallen off
Basidia
Spores
Young Spores
Central Tissue

*Fig. 6 Spore germinating (x 300)*
*(a)* *(b)* *(c)*

*Fig. 7 Germinating Sclerotium in longitudinal Section*
Spore fruit with an Investment
Sclerotium

*Fig. 8 Female Plant of Polysiphonia*

RED SEA WEED
*Fig. 9 Growing points of Plocamium*
*(a)*
*(b) more highly magnified*
Growing Point

*Fig. 10 Tetragonidia of Polysiphonia*
Tetragonidia
Spaces from which Tetragonidia have escaped

*Fig. 11 Successive Stages of development of Tetragonidium*
*a* *b* *c* *d* *e*

Engraved, Printed and Published by W. & A.K. Johnston, Edinburgh.

PLATE XVIII.

# RED SEA-WEED (*Polysiphonia Subulata*)—*continued.*

*Fig. 1* Male Plant.
Antheridia, or male sexual organs, are cone-like, supported by a short stalk. Forked hair on the outside of each protecting it.
*Fig. 1a* Ripe Antheridium in optical section (× 430).
There is a basal-cell forming the Stalk, a row of cells in the centre forming an Axis, and the mother-cells of the Antherozoids are grouped around this Axis. The Antherozoids are spherical motionless masses of protoplasm, discharged into the surrounding water by the bursting of the ripe mother-cell.
*Figs. 2 and 3* Female Plant.
Carpogonia, or female sexual organs, are obovate, when ready for fertilisation, and consist of three principal parts—
1. Foot or attachment.
2. Fertile spore-forming part. This is the swollen portion, and consists of a central cell surrounded by a number of peripheral cells.

3. Hair apparatus, consisting of the forked hair and the Trichogyne (Gr. *trichos,* hair; *gone,* seed).
*Fig. 4* The process of Fertilisation is extremely interesting, because of the part that Infusoria have recently been found to play in it. The antherozoids, discharged into the surrounding sea-water by the bursting of the ripe antheridia, are passively floated about by the waves, since they are motionless in themselves, and they may accidentally come into contact with the trichogyne of a female plant; but their chances are greatly increased by the action of unconscious agents, such as Infusoria, which create currents in the water in the neighbourhood of the female organs. Vorticella, or the Bell Animalcule, is a stalked Infusorian, attached to this red sea-weed. The stalk may either be lengthened out, as in the drawing, or shortened by being coiled into a spiral. The bell is surmounted by a crown of cilia which move in a

definite order, so as to cause currents which will sweep particles of food down the gullet. The Vorticella is at first a free-swimming unstalked bell, but with the stalk it becomes fixed, and it naturally settles down where their is likely to be an abundance of food. The currents set up necessarily send antherozoids down the gullet, but some come in contact with the apex of the trichogyne, and are retained there. The forked hair, too, will serve to break the force of the current, and form a sort of eddy, so that the antherozoids may the more readily settle down where wanted. The antherozoid thus blends with the trichogyne, and its substance passes down the canal of the trichogyne, till it reaches the central cell, and thus fertilisation is effected.
The forked hair and trichogyne both disappear after fertilisation, having served their purpose.

*Life History.*—The Red Sea-weeds multiply by a simple non-sexual process, or are reproduced sexually in a complicated manner.

The contents of certain cells break up into four portions, which escape by rupturing the cell-wall, and germinating reproduce the parent plant. These are the Tetragonidia produced non-sexually.

In some red sea-weeds the male and female organs are on different parts of the same plant, but in Polysiphonia they are on different plants. The Male plant produces Antheridia, which begin as a single-celled branch, then become a row of cells, and finally a cone-like mass of cells. The forked hair arises from the stalk-cell, and the other cells produce the rounded Antherozoids. The Female plant produces Oogonia, but as they become spore-fruits after fertilisation, they are called Carpogonia. These arise, like the Antheridia, from a single cell, which eventually becomes a basal portion or Foot, consisting of a ring of four cells, and one in the centre; a middle or Fertile portion, consisting of a large central cell, surrounded by a number of cells ; and a top portion, consisting of a long cell or Trichogyne, with a forked hair. An Antherozoid reaching the apex of the trichogyne, in the way already described, is retained there, and strange to say, the fertilising effect is produced at some distance in the central cell and surrounding cells of the Carpogonium. The surrounding cells grow and divide till they form a fruit-like cover, while the central cell forms a number of close.set branches, at the ends of which the Carpospores are developed. There is thus a Spore-fruit formed, which discharges its so-called Carpospores or Endogonidia by a hole at the top; these on germination give rise to young plants.

PLATE XX.

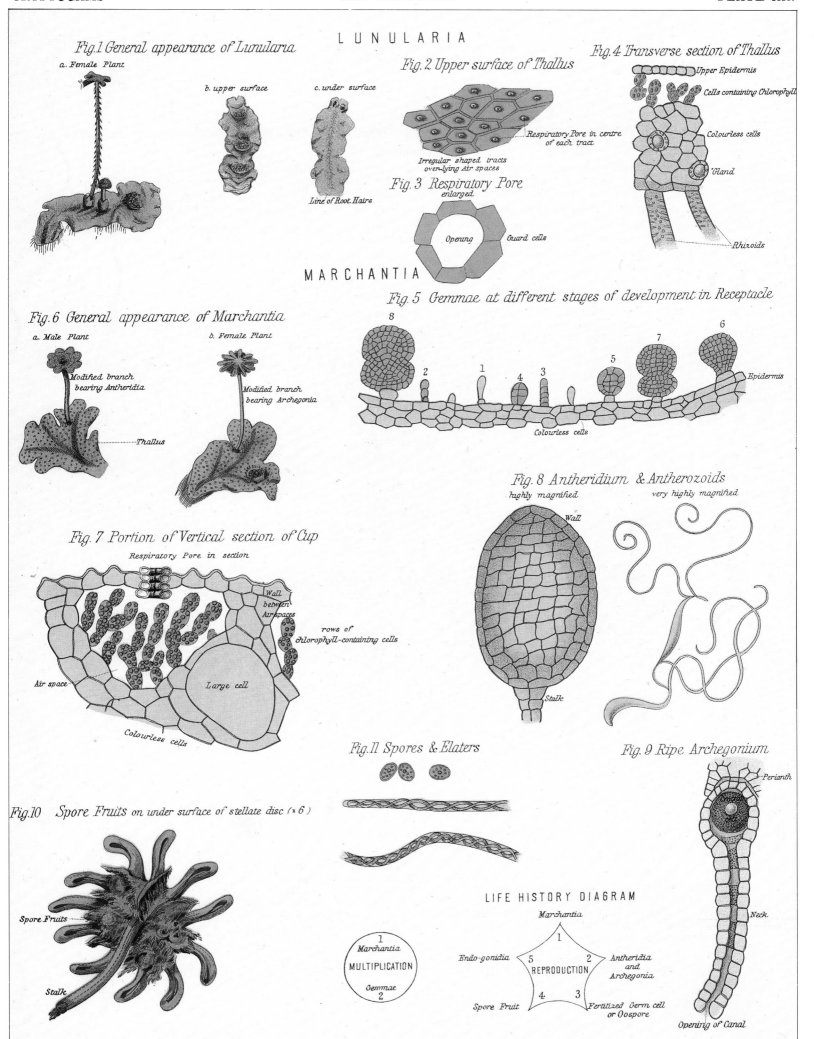

LUNULARIA

Fig.1 General appearance of Lunularia
a. Female Plant
b. upper surface
c. under surface
Line of Root Hairs

Fig.2 Upper surface of Thallus
Respiratory Pore in centre of each tract
Irregular shaped tracts over-lying Air spaces

Fig.3 Respiratory Pore enlarged
Opening
Guard cells

Fig.4 Transverse section of Thallus
Upper Epidermis
Cells containing Chlorophyll
Colourless cells
Gland
Rhizoids

MARCHANTIA

Fig.5 Gemmae at different stages of development in Receptacle
Epidermis
Colourless cells

Fig.6 General appearance of Marchantia
a. Male Plant
Modified branch bearing Antheridia
b. Female Plant
Modified branch bearing Archegonia
Thallus

Fig.8 Antheridium & Antherozoids
highly magnified
very highly magnified
Wall
Stalk

Fig.7 Portion of Vertical section of Cup
Respiratory Pore in section
Wall between Air spaces
rows of chlorophyll-containing cells
Air space
Large cell
Colourless cells

Fig.11 Spores & Elaters

Fig.9 Ripe Archegonium
Perianth
Neck
Opening of Canal

Fig.10 Spore Fruits on under surface of stellate disc (× 6)
Spore Fruits
Stalk

LIFE HISTORY DIAGRAM

Marchantia
1
Marchantia MULTIPLICATION Gemmae
2

Marchantia
1
Endo-gonidia 5 REPRODUCTION 2 Antheridia and Archegonia
Spore Fruit 4 3 Fertilized Germ cell or Oospore

Engraved, Printed and Published by W. & A.K. Johnston, Edinburgh.

PLATE XXI.
# COMMON HAIR-MOSS (*Polytrichum*) and FUNARIA HYGROMETRICA.

Mosses are common everywhere, on wall-tops, roofs, and trees, decking the banks with a mantle of green, or carpeting the forests with their luxuriance. Mosses, however, like other plants, have also their favourite haunts and their favourite seasons, but Funaria has this advantage, that it may be found in fruit at almost any season of the year.

The Hair-Moss (*Polytrichum*) is common on waste-ground and heaths where it forms tufted masses. The male and female organs are borne by distinct plants, and the hairy cap of the moss-fruit may be readily recognised. The stem may be several inches in height.

Funaria occurs on walls, roofs, and waste-places pretty common. The leafy plant is small, but the stalk bearing the pear-shaped capsule is an inch or two in length. This stalk has the peculiarity of contracting to a spiral on drying after being moistened.

*Fig. 1* Male Plant of Polytrichum, with numerous brown root-hairs and slender stem.
The apex of the stem forms a leafy expansion bearing the male organs.
*Fig. 2* Female plant of Funaria.
In the young condition the Capsule is sessile, but it is borne on a long stalk later.
The Leafy plant has a very short stem, with bright green leaves overlapping each other.
*Fig. 3* The flattened apex is bounded by leaves, and bears stalked bodies of considerable size intermixed with barren filaments.
The stalked bodies are the male organs or Antheridia, consisting of a wall formed of a single layer of cells, and the interior cells developing Antherozoids.
Tease out portions of the apex, and examine under high power for

Antheridia with Antherozoids, and Archegonia.
*Fig. 4* Antherozoid, a coiled body with two cilia. Stain with iodine to kill them and make cilia visible.
*Fig. 5* Archegonium a flask shaped body with long neck and a lower swollen portion containing the central cell.
*Fig. 6* Sporocarp of Polytrichum.
The unripe Capsule is still green and covered by its brown hairy cap.
The lid beneath the cap is peaked.
The ripe Capsule is of a brownish-yellow and the cap yellowish.
*Fig. 7* Ripe Spore-capsule of Polytrichum (June).
The lid is cast off and the spores escape.
The mouth of the capsule is surrounded by sixty-four teeth forming the Peristome.

The Epiphragm is the expanded end of the Columella.
*Fig. 8* Peristome of Funaria consisting of sixteen teeth converging to a centre.
*Fig. 9* Embed Capsules of Funaria in paraffin, and make longitudinal and transverse sections.
Outer wall or peripheral layer of cells.
Columella or central cylinder of colourless cells.
Spore-sac surrounding columella.
Air-cavity with strings of green cells permeating through it.
*Fig. 10* Ripe spore consisting of inner and outer wall, protoplasm and oil-globules.
*Fig. 11* Sow spores on blotting-paper kept moist under a glass shade.
*Fig. 12* The germinating spore gives rise to a thread-like branching body the Protonema, and a bud forms which grows up into the leafy Moss.

*Life History of a Moss.* — The leafy Moss-plant forms at its apex either Antheridia producing Antherozoids or Archegonia with their Central-cells. The antherozoids fertilise the central cell, converting it into an Oospore. This oospore divides and produces directly the Sporogonium with its contained Spores. The top of the ripe capsule detaches itself, and the spores come out : and on a suitable .situation begin to germinate. The thick outer coat is ruptured, and the inner coat protrudes as a filament which grows, divides and branches, till a mass of branched filaments is formed called the Protonema. The Protonema gives rise to a bud by the bulging out of a side branch, and this produces the leafy Moss as at the beginning.

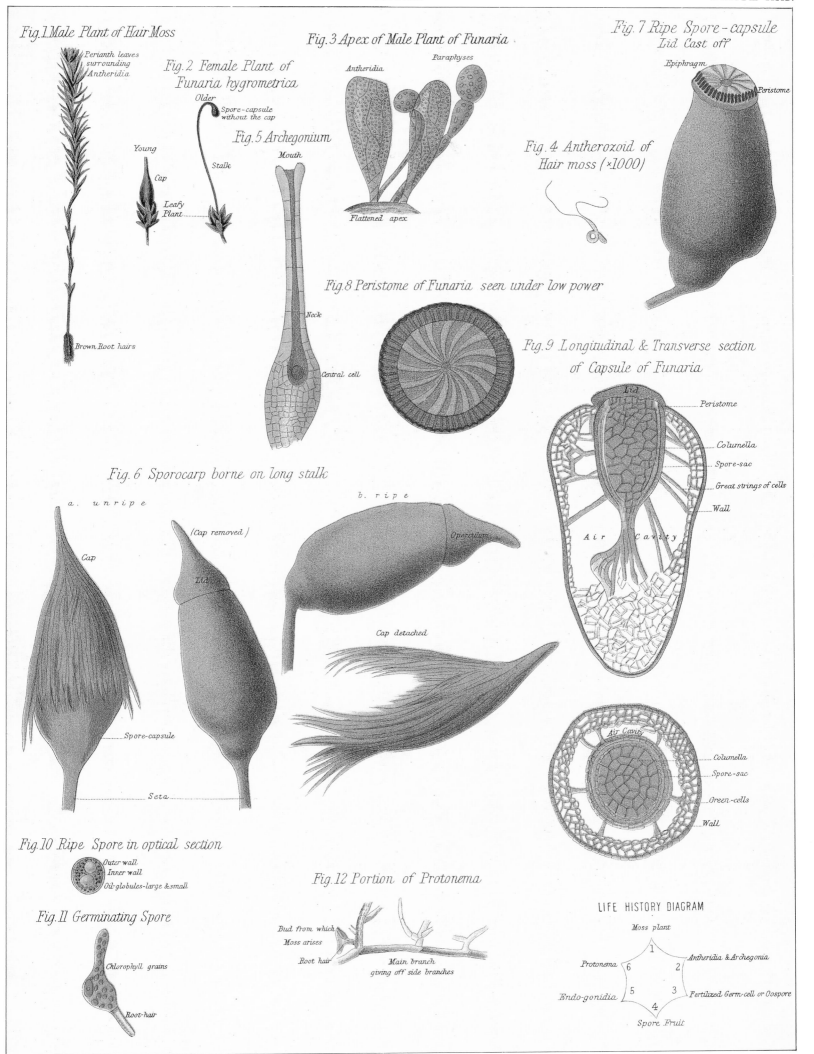

Fig. 1 Male Plant of Hair Moss

Perianth leaves surrounding Antheridia

Brown Root hairs

Fig. 2 Female Plant of Funaria hygrometrica

Older
Spore-capsule without the cap

Young
Cap
Leafy Plant
Stalk

Fig. 3 Apex of Male Plant of Funaria

Antheridia
Paraphyses
Flattened apex

Fig. 5 Archegonium

Mouth
Neck
Central cell

Fig. 4 Antherozoid of Hair moss (×1000)

Fig. 7 Ripe Spore-capsule Lid Cast off

Epiphragm
Peristome

Fig. 8 Peristome of Funaria seen under low power

Fig. 9 Longitudinal & Transverse section of Capsule of Funaria

Lid
Peristome
Columella
Spore-sac
Great strings of cells
Wall
Air Cavity

Air Cavity
Columella
Spore-sac
Green-cells
Wall

Fig. 6 Sporocarp borne on long stalk

a. unripe
Cap
Spore-capsule
Seta

(Cap removed)
Lid

b. ripe
Operculum
Cap detached

Fig. 10 Ripe Spore in optical section

Outer wall
Inner wall
Oil-globules-large & small

Fig. 11 Germinating Spore

Chlorophyll grains
Root-hair

Fig. 12 Portion of Protonema

Bud from which Moss arises
Root hair
Main branch giving off side branches

LIFE HISTORY DIAGRAM

Moss plant
Protonema
Antheridia & Archegonia
Endo-gonidia
Fertilized Germ-cell or Oospore
Spore Fruit
1  2  3  4  5  6

Engraved, Printed and Published by W. & A.K. Johnston, Edinburgh.

PLATE XXII.

# MALE SHIELD FERN (*Aspidium filix-mas*).

Ferns have always attracted notice from their graceful outlines and their varied forms, still it is only comparatively recently that the complete course of their life history has been made out. The frond of the Fern is the most conspicuous, the underground portion being generally overlooked. Having so much leaf about them, they generally inhabit moist and shady situations. Their prevailing colour is green, but towards the autumn a brown hue appears on the under surface of the frond, in streaks or patches, and this is due to the formation of spore-cases containing the spores.

The Male Shield Fern is so named by way of contrast to an allied form—the Lady Fern, with its graceful habit, its elegant form, and its delicate hue. It bears its fronds in tufts, arranged in shuttle-cock fashion, and rising to a height of two or three feet. The young fronds are rolled up like a shepherd's crook, and gradually unfold themselves. The veining of the leaflets is distinctly seen, and that constant forking of the veins so characteristic of Ferns. The spore-cases are arranged in patches, each patch being indicated by its kidney-shaped cover. The amount of spores produced is enormous, and readily accounts for its extensive distribution. Professor Dodel-Port has reckoned the number of spores scattered by a single fern, in a single summer, to be no less than one thousand millions.

*Fig. 1* Underground Stem ascends obliquely, and is completely covered with the stumps of leaves, from the base of which the numerous roots arise.

*Fig. 2* Fertile leaf or frond bearing Sporangia on under surface.
The leaf is bi-pinnate; the pinnae are long, narrow, tapering, and the pinnules are obtuse.
On the under surface of the leaf, usually at the forking of two veins, kidney-shaped structures appear called Indusia. Each Indusium covers a cluster of stalked capsules, such a cluster being called a Sorus, and each stalked capsule a Sporangium.

*Fig. 3* Pinna or leaflet on upper surface.

The pinnules towards the top run into each other.
The forked Venation is evident.

*Fig. 4* Pinnule from base of Pinna.
The Indusium may be found *closed* over the cluster of Sporangia, or *raised* on one side to allow the ripe spores to escape, or in some cases *burst*.

*Fig. 5* Section of Pinnule through Ripe Sorus in Fig. 4. Indusium arising from central swelling of vascular bundle, arching completely over clusters of Sporangia, and consisting of a single layer of nucleated cells in its expanded portions.
Sporangia in different stages of development, opened and unopened, full and empty of Spores. Some have longer or shorter stalks, with a stalked gland which is peculiar to the species, and there are several hair-like undeveloped Sporangia known as Paraphyses.

*Fig. 6* The Sporangia may be rubbed off on a slide and examined in water. They can afterwards be burst by pressure on the cover-glass.
The Sporangium is an oval body borne by a short stalk. There is a ring of thick projecting cells extending from the cleft overhead, and backwards to the top of the stalk. The cells forming the slightly convex wall on either side are thin and easily ruptured.

*Fig. 7* Spores.
The Spore has a thick, outer brown coat or Exosporium with irregular markings, and a thin, inner delicate coat or Endosporium.

## PLATE XXV.

## COMMON CLUB-MOSS (*Lycopodium clavatum*)
## and *Selaginella*.

*(Chiefly from Luerssen's "Medicinisch Pharmaceutische Botanik.")*

### LYCOPODIUM.

Club-mosses, as the common name denotes are moss-like plants, having slender herbaceous stems, clothed with delicate small leaves, and found in mountainous situations or stony, wet places.

The fossil forms of the Carboniferous period, of which Lepidodendron is the most characteristic, instead of being herbaceous, were large trees.

The prostrate creeping Stem is very leafy, and much branched. From the under surface arise the roots, and from the upper surface the upright fertile shoots, ending generally in two fertile spikes.

The Leaves are hair-pointed, and arranged in a close spiral round the stem.

The Modified Leaves bearing the sporangia are shorter and broader than the ordinary leaves, though sometimes they are quite the same.

The numerous minute spores (Fig. 4) are applied to various uses. They contain a quantity of resinous matter, and their wall is of a greasy nature. This resinous quality renders them readily combustible, hence they are used as "vegetable sulphur" for producing an artificial and sudden flame to represent lightning at theatres, and their greasy coat has caused them to be used for dusting over pills, thus preventing the contained pill from touching the tongue.

*Fig. 1* Creeping Stem branches dichotomously, and also the Roots. Leaves thickly set round the stem. Spikes usually in pairs, mounted on a stalk.
*Fig. 2* Leaf one-nerved and irregularly toothed, with a long hair-point variable in length.
*Fig. 3* Fertile leaf bearing Sporangium at its base on the upper surface. Sporangium kidney-shaped, splitting into two valves, and producing only one kind of spore.
*Fig. 4* Spore with netted markings fading away towards apex. Three converging ridges, along which exospore ruptures.
*Fig. 5* Prothallus of Lycopodium, discovered by Fankhauser in the autumn of 1872.
It is an underground solid structure, without chlorophyll, pretty smooth on the under surface, but deeply grooved on the upper. Antheridia and Archegonia are developed in the grooves.

*Life History Diagram.*—The discovery of the Prothallus shows that the Lycopod, in its reproductive processes, is more nearly allied to Ferns, such as Adder's tongue (*Ophioglossum*), than to Selaginella, beside which its vegetative characters seemed to place it.

The fertile leaves of the spike bear sporangia on their inner base, the spores of which are of one kind. The spore on germination produces a prothallus, underground, solid, without chlorophyll, independent of the spore, and with Antheridia and Archegonia. The embryo resulting from fertilization forms a foot embedded in the tissue of the prothallus, and grows up into the young plant.

### CLASSIFICATION OF LYCOPODIUM.

*Sub-kingdom.* Vascular Cryptogams.

*Class.* Dichotomæ.
Stem and Roots branching dichotomously.
Leaves small and simple.

Sporangia solitary.
Spores of one or two kinds.
*Order.* Lycopodiaceæ.
Leaves without a ligule.
Spores of one kind.
Prothallus large and independent.

*Genus.* Lycopodium, only British genus.

*Species.* Clavatum.
Spikes usually in pairs, long-stalked.

### SELAGINELLA.

Selaginella, with only one British species, the lesser Club-moss, has a special interest from the fact that it not only belongs to the highest group of Cryptogams, but that it shows a gradual passage from the reproductive processes characteristic of Cryptogams to those of Phanerogams. It is this phase of its character which will receive special attention now.

The Reproductive Structures are of two kinds, and, generally speaking, the Macrosporangia are only produced on the lower leaves, and Microsporangia on the upper. In Pilularia, Sporangia of two kinds were produced, springing in tufts from the inner (or upper) surface of four modified leaves arranged in a whorl, but here they spring singly and separately from the upper surface of leaves arranged spirally. In the one case the leaves were all at one level, united at their edges, and *enclosing* the Sporangia, here the leaves are drawn out into a spiral, and bear the Sporangia without enclosing them.

The developing Embryo (as in Fig. 14) will show the points of contact with higher plants. For the first time there appears in the spore, along with the female prothallus, yet distinct from it, a mass of cells which supply nutriment to the young and growing embryo. This is the *Endosperm* of higher plants. Further, the embryo as soon as it forms the rudiments

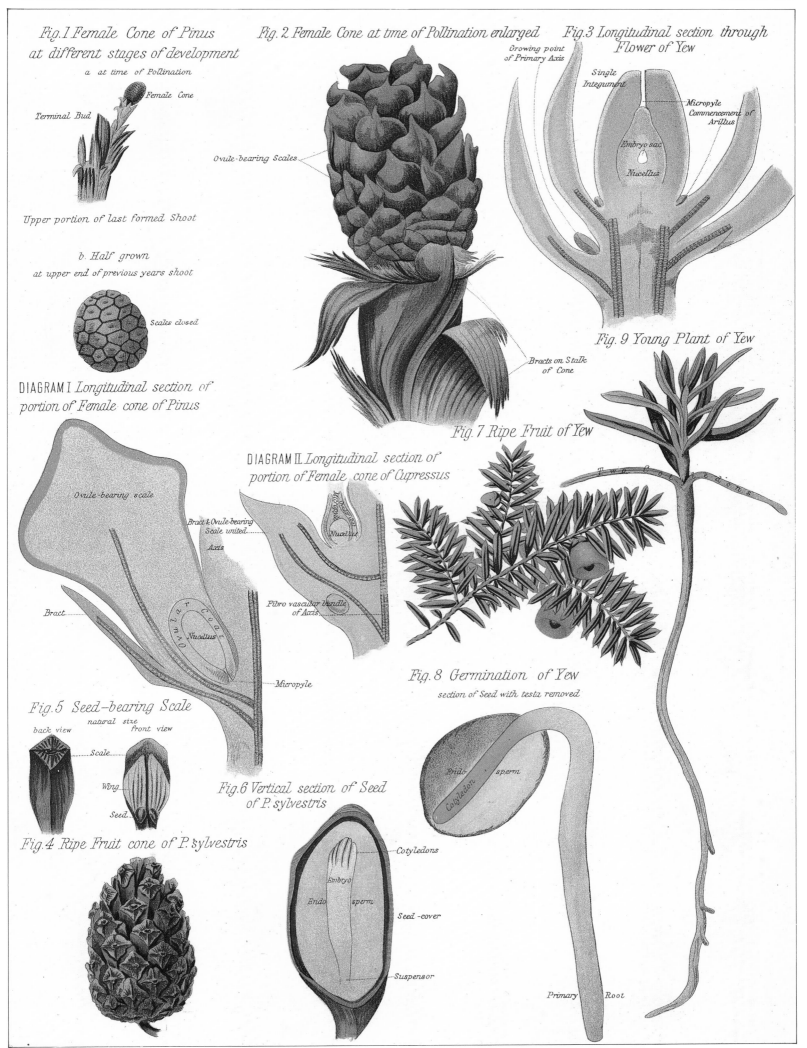

Fig.1 Female Cone of Pinus at different stages of development

a at time of Pollination

Female Cone

Terminal Bud

Upper portion of last formed Shoot

b. Half grown at upper end of previous years shoot

Scales closed

DIAGRAM I Longitudinal section of portion of Female cone of Pinus

Ovule-bearing scale

Bract & Ovule-bearing Scale united

Axis

Ovular Coat

Nucellus

Bract

Micropyle

Fig.5 Seed-bearing Scale

back view   natural size   front view

Scale

Wing

Seed

Fig.4 Ripe Fruit cone of P. sylvestris

Fig.2 Female Cone at time of Pollination enlarged

Ovule-bearing Scales

Bracts on Stalk of Cone

Fig.7 Ripe Fruit of Yew

DIAGRAM II. Longitudinal section of portion of Female cone of Cupressus

Micropyle

Nucellus

Fibro vascular bundle of Axis

Fig.6 Vertical section of Seed of P. sylvestris

Cotyledons

Embryo

Endo sperm

Seed-cover

Suspensor

Fig.3 Longitudinal section through Flower of Yew

Growing point of Primary Axis

Single Integument

Micropyle Commencement of Arillus

Embryo sac

Nucellus

Fig. 9 Young Plant of Yew

Two Cotyledons

Fig.8 Germination of Yew

section of Seed with testa removed

Endo sperm

Cotyledon

Primary   Root

Engraved, Printed and Published by W. & A.K. Johnston, Edinburgh.

PLATE IV.

# ANNUAL MEADOW GRASS (*Poa annua*) and
# SAND CAREX (*Carex arenaria*).

## GRASS.

The Grass chosen is common everywhere by the road-side, and may be had in flower at almost any season of the year. The flower is exceedingly small, and when the season permits the flower of Wheat might be examined instead.

Grasses are usually wind-fertilised—the pollen is wafted from flower, to flower, and thus there is an interchange of pollen. In accordance with this arrangement, the flower is inconspicuous and without gaudy colours, the anthers hang out on long filaments and turn about with every breath of wind, and the stigma is a branching tree, in miniature, to entangle the pollen as it passes.

Some, however, are self-fertilised—and the Annual Meadow Grass is an example.

*Fig. 1* General characters.
Root, fibrous.
Stem, hollow and jointed. In the quickly growing stem, the outer parts grow faster than the inner, so that the interior is ruptured and a hollow produced. The fibro-vascular bundles form a horizontal partition at the nodes, and thus strengthen the stem.
Leaves, linear and alternate, with pointed membranous Ligule at junction of sheath and blade.
Inflorescence consisting of an axis with branches bearing stalked flowers. Spikelet composed of several flowers.
*Fig. 2* Spikelet detached.
There are two bracts at the base, imbricating with each other, and the axis of the spikelet bears the flowers.
*Fig. 3* Floret detached.
The Stigma in the centre is seen to be branched and hairy in order to intercept and retain the pollen.
The Anthers are placed on slender filaments.
The Flowering glume and Pale are simply bracts overlapping each other.
*Fig. 4* Under the dissecting microscope detach the different parts

of the flower, by steadying it with needle in left hand and removing parts with cutting needle in right. Remove the flowering glume and two little scales will be seen side by side, embracing ovary opposite to pale, and one stamen coming out between them. Great care and steadiness of hand are required in removing these entire, so that they may be laid out and examined.
The Flower is extremely simple, consisting of two little scales, three Stamens, and two Carpels, as indicated by the two Stigmas—
Little scales or Lodicules probably representing a Perianth.
Stamens three, alternating with lodicules. The anthers hang down because the filaments are weak.
Carpels consisting of swollen Ovary, crowned by two diverging feathery Stigmas.
*Diagram* I.—Plan of flower, showing the parts at one level and in their proper relations.
Perianth of two free segments.
Androecium of three Stamens.

Gynoecium of two united Carpels.
*Diagram* II.—By comparing a number of flowers it is possible to construct a theoretical diagram, showing the flower of which grass may be a reduced form. In the Rice flower, for instance, there are two rows of stamens of three each.
This diagram will be seen to agree with that of the Lily in the following Plate.
*Fig. 5* Ovary with spreading Stigmas.
*Figs. 6 and 7* Grains of wheat soaked in water and sections made.
Embryo is at base of seed, and the rest filled up with mealy Endosperm.
*Fig. 8* Place a few grains of wheat in flannel, keep moist and at a moderate temperature, and germination will soon begin.
*Fig. 9* Root-hairs.
On young roots, the cells of the epidermis are drawn out into delicate root-hairs. These root-hairs being so thin are extremely permeable to fluids, and it is through them the root withdraws from the soil the necessary plant-food.

## SEDGE (from *Luerssen*).

Sedges may be contrasted in their general structure with Grasses. The Stem is solid and usually triangular. The Leaves are arranged in three rows on the stem and the sheath is not split. The Flowers are developed in scale-like bracts called glumes, as in grasses, but are usually male and female, and not bi-sexual like the flower of Grass. Sedges are mostly found in damp places.

*Fig. 10* Triangular Stem.
*Fig. 11* Spike bearing Female spikelets at bottom, female and male spikelets about middle, and entirely Male spikelets at top.
*Fig. 12* and *Diagram* III.—Male Flower consisting simply of three Stamens enclosed by a bract.
*Fig. 13* and *Diagram* IV.—Female

Flower consisting of two united Carpels, and the bracteole has grown completely round, enclosing it as in a bottle.
*Fig. 14* Fruit is of a chestnut colour, and invested by the enlarged bracteole.
*Diagram* V.—In *Carex* the flower is seen to be really borne on an aborted

axis, which arises in the axil of the outer bract.
In *Elyna* this axis is seen to develop further, producing not only a Female but also a Male Flower.
The apparently single flower in the case of Carex would thus seem to be a reduced Inflorescence.

## CLASSIFICATION.

*Group*. Angiosperms.
Ovules enclosed in an Ovary.
Endosperm, not formed in Embryo-sac before fertilisation.

*Class*. Monocotyledon.
Leaves with parallel veins.
Parts of Flower in threes.
Embryo with one Seed-leaf or Cotyledon.

*Order*. Graminaceæ.
Stem, hollow.
Leaves, alternate, with split sheaths, and ligules at junction of blade and sheath.
Flowers, in scaly bracts.
Stamens, three, and anthers versatile.
Stigmas, two, and feathery.
Fruit, dry, and one-seeded.

Seed with Endosperm.
*Order*. Cyperaceæ.
Stem, solid and triangular.
Leaves, with unsplit sheaths and no ligule.
Flowers, in scaly bracts.
Stamens, one to three.
Stigmas, two or three.
Fruit, dry, and one-seeded.
Seed with Endosperm.

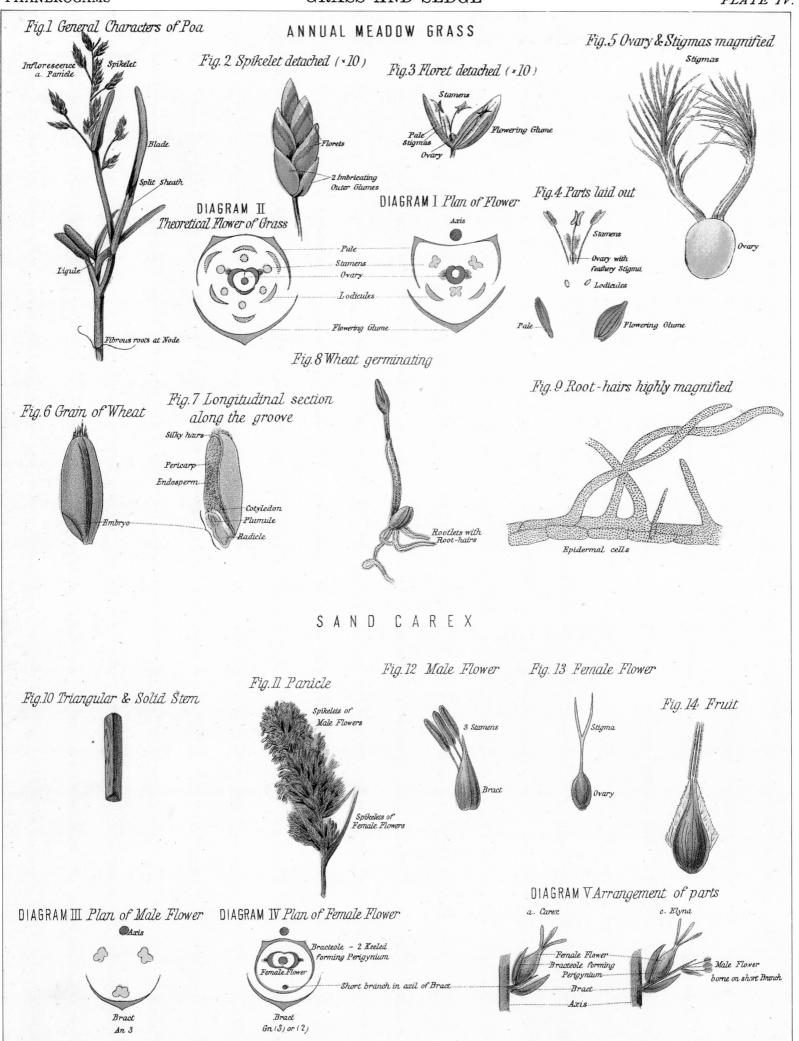

ANNUAL MEADOW GRASS

Fig.1 General Characters of Poa

Inflorescence a. Panicle
Spikelet
Blade
Split Sheath
Ligule
Fibrous roots at Node

Fig.2 Spikelet detached (×10)

Florets
2 Imbricating Outer Glumes

DIAGRAM II
Theoretical Flower of Grass

Pale
Stamens
Ovary
Lodicules
Flowering Glume

Fig.3 Floret detached (×10)

Stamens
Pale
Stigmas
Ovary
Flowering Glume

DIAGRAM I Plan of Flower

Axis

Fig.4 Parts laid out

Stamens
Ovary with feathery Stigma
Lodicules
Pale
Flowering Glume

Fig.5 Ovary & Stigmas magnified

Stigmas
Ovary

Fig.8 Wheat germinating

Fig.6 Grain of Wheat

Fig.7 Longitudinal section along the groove

Silky hairs
Pericarp
Endosperm
Embryo
Cotyledon
Plumule
Radicle

Rootlets with Root-hairs

Fig.9 Root-hairs highly magnified

Epidermal cells

SAND CAREX

Fig.10 Triangular & Solid Stem

Fig.11 Panicle

Spikelets of Male Flowers
Spikelets of Female Flowers

Fig.12 Male Flower

3 Stamens
Bract

Fig.13 Female Flower

Stigma
Ovary

Fig.14 Fruit

DIAGRAM V Arrangement of parts

a. Carex
c. Elyna

Female Flower
Bracteole forming Perigynium
Bract
Axis
Male Flower borne on short Branch

DIAGRAM III Plan of Male Flower

Axis
Bract
An 3

DIAGRAM IV Plan of Female Flower

Bracteole - 2 Keeled forming Perigynium
Female Flower
Short branch in axil of Bract
Bract
Gn (3) or (2)

Engraved, Printed and Published by W. & A.K. Johnston, Edinburgh.

PLATE V.

# MARTAGON LILY (*Lilium Martagon*) and CROWN IMPERIAL (*Fritillaria imperialis*).

*(Figs. 1, 8 and 9 after Dodel-Port.)*

The flowers hitherto considered have all been rather sombre in their tints. In the case of the Coniferæ there were no brilliant or gaudy colours, but the flowers were hidden, as it were, out of sight with a covering of scales. The Grasses and Sedges, too, had their minute flowers of a greenish or brownish tint, and everything betokened business, but no attempt at decoration.

But when we come to Lilies and such like, the beauty of their flowers form the most striking feature, often with further attractions in the shape of perfume and honey. This change from grave to gay, to sweetness and scent, has probably reference to the visits of insects; and now, instead of the pollen being scattered by the wind with extravagant wastefulness, a more economical method has been found in the agency of insects. Insects are attracted first of all by the colour and scent, then honey is provided, so that in obtaining it they may carry the pollen of one flower to the stigma of another, and thus unconsciously, while pursuing their own selfish ends, effect cross-fertilisation, which enables the plant to produce a stronger and healthier progeny than otherwise.

The Nectary consists of a tissue, formed of small, thin-walled cells, from which sweet juices exude and keep it constantly moist. They are generally placed in the recesses of the flower, and in the present instance occupy the base of the perianth-leaves.

The Martagon Lily is an instance of a *regular* Monocotyledon flower adapted for cross-fertilisation by insects, although in the absence of insects it may be self-fertilised.

*Fig. 1* Flower of Martagon Lily fully developed.
The flower in the bud condition has its various parts arranged, as in Fritillaria (Fig. 2). The coloured leaves are directed downwards, enclosing the straight stamens and style; but as the flower expands these different parts diverge, until finally the coloured leaves curl upwards and meet around the stalk; the stamens spread out like a fan, and the style curves in the direction of most light. The nectaries, at the base of the coloured leaves, secrete drops of honey, and the anthers open to discharge their pollen. If, now, an insect visits the flower, alighting on the spread-out stamens, as a convenient resting-place, while sipping the honey with its long proboscis, it will carry away pollen on various parts of its body, and likely leave some of it on the stigma of the next flower it visits.

*Figs. 2 and 3* Fritillaria has been halved lengthwise in its natural pendent position, and the six nectaries are seen at the base of the perianth-leaves in Fig. 3.
*Diagram I.*—Plan of Flower, representing typical Monocotyledon. Calyx or outer whorl of three free Sepals. Corolla or inner whorl of three free Petals, alternating with the Sepals.

When the parts of the Calyx and Corolla are similar in size, shape, and colour, it is usual to call them collectively the Perianth. The Nectaries are at the base of each perianth-leaf.

Andrœcium of two whorls of three Stamens each.
Gynœcium of three united Carpels.

*Figs. 4 and 5* The Foliage-leaves get smaller on ascending the stem, till you pass by regular gradations into the bracts at the base of the flower-stalks.
*Fig. 6* Stamen.
The Anther appears at first to be quite in line with the Filament, but as the stamen curves outwards, the anther comes to swing on the very top of the filament, so as readily to discharge its contents (as in Fig. I).
*Figs. 7 and 8* Each Anther-lobe consists of two pollen-sacs, and opens by a longitudinal slit down the side.
*Fig. 9* The Pollen-grain of Mantagon Lily is a striking example of beauty and utility combined. It is beautifully netted on the outer surface, and each mesh of the net usually contains a globule of oil. This oil is to keep it moist until it reaches the stigma with its secretion, and the netted arrangement distributes the oil more evenly and generally over the surface.

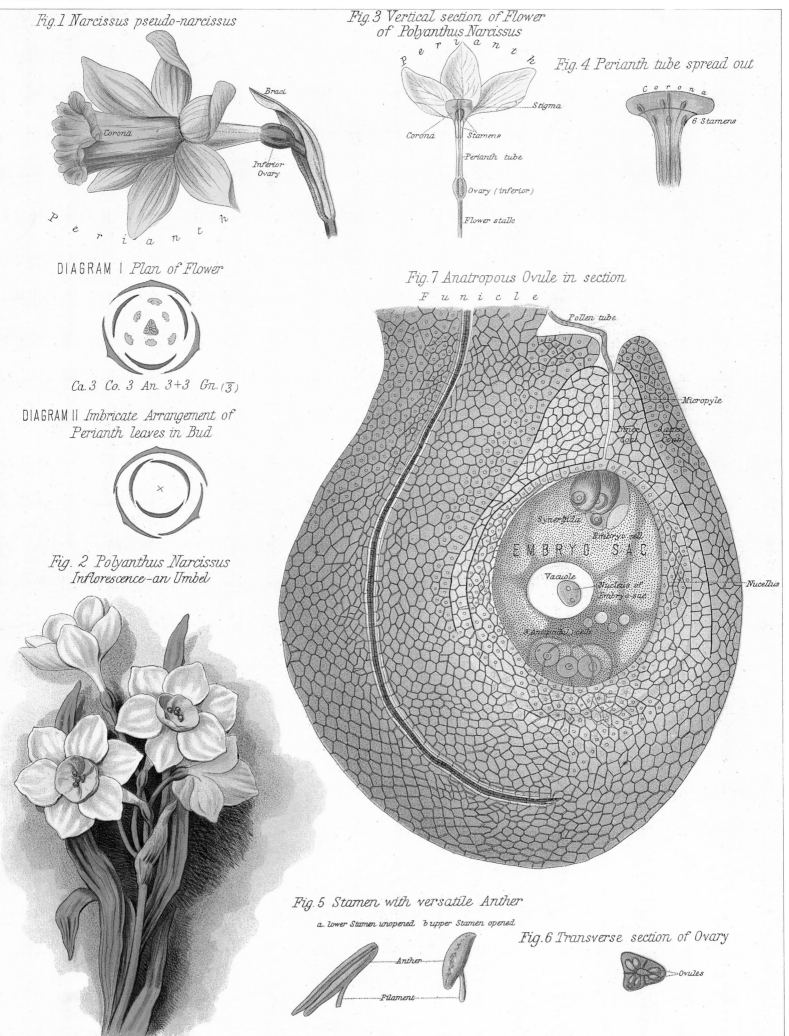

Fig.1 Narcissus pseudo-narcissus

Corona

Perianth

Bract

Inferior Ovary

Fig.3 Vertical section of Flower of Polyanthus Narcissus

Perianth

Stigma

Corona

Stamens

Perianth tube

Ovary (inferior)

Flower stalk

Fig.4 Perianth tube spread out

Corona

6 Stamens

DIAGRAM I Plan of Flower

Ca. 3  Co. 3  An. 3+3  Gn. (3̄)

DIAGRAM II Imbricate Arrangement of Perianth leaves in Bud

Fig. 2 Polyanthus Narcissus Inflorescence-an Umbel

Fig.7 Anatropous Ovule in section

Funicle

Pollen tube

Micropyle

Synergida

Embryo cell

EMBRYO SAC

Vacuole

Nucleus of Embryo sac

Nucellus

3 Antipodal cells

Fig.5 Stamen with versatile Anther

a. lower Stamen unopened   b upper Stamen opened

Anther

Filament

Fig.6 Transverse section of Ovary

Ovules

Engraved, Printed and Published by W. & A.K. Johnston, Edinburgh.

PLATE VIII.

# CROCUS.

The Crocus, the Gladiolus, and the Iris are well-known members of a family, prized for their large and showy flowers, which vie with the rainbow in their hues. Yellow, blue, purple, and crimson are the prevailing colours.

The Crocus comes to us as the harbinger of spring, and forms a very good introduction to that wealth of floral display which is continued onwards almost to the close of the year. But it has not merely beauty to recommend it, for the Saffron or *Crocus sativus*, which has been cultivated for centuries yields that beautiful yellow colouring matter which is used for dyeing, for flavouring soups, and also in medicine. It is from the stigmas, which are of a deep orange-red colour passing into yellow, that the dye is obtained. This order is characterised by having three stamens, the anthers of which open outwards, and the stigmas usually petaloid.

*Figs. 1 and 2* Two different flowers are represented to show the relative position of Stigma and Anther in each case.

Fig. 1 shows the expanded stigmas projecting above the Anthers, while Fig. 2 shows the mature Anthers at the mouth of the perianth-tube, the stigmas being lower down.

*Fig 3* Perianth of six Segments uniting below to form a long slender tube.

*Fig. 4* Detach flower from underground stem, and slit it up from below.

Flower-stalk, relatively short. Perianth-tube, expanding into the showy Segments. The Segments are usually equal, but in this particular instance they were as indicated. Ovary, underground, and Ovules arranged around a central axis. The Ovary is *apparently* inferior and the Perianth superior, but as the ovary ripens the Perianth-tube is clearly seen to arise from the base of the ovary, as in Fig. 9.

The ovules are fertilised while still underground, but the flower stalk afterwards lengthens, thus raising the Ovary above ground where the ripening of the seeds is completed. Style, long and filamentous, usually projecting from the tube and ending in the three-lobed Stigma.

*Diagrams* I. and II.—Examine young Crocus, and make out spiral arrangement of Perianth-leaves as in Diag. II.

## PLAN OF FLOWER

Calyx of three coloured Sepals, united at base to form a tube.
Corolla of three coloured Petals,
Androecium of three Stamens inserted at the base of the three outer segments of the Perianth.
Gynoecium of three united Carpels.

*Fig. 5* The underground Stem is distinguished as a Corm (Lat. *cormus*, a solid bulb), because the swollen portion is chiefly composed of stem, whereas in the Bulb it is composed largely of the swollen bases of leaves as well.

*Fig. 6* Foliage-leaves, long, narrow and pointed, with a *furrow* running along the middle, and a corresponding *ridge* on the opposite side.

This is well seen in a transverse section of the leaf.

*Fig. 7* Stamen—the Filament is flattened, and the Anther is arrow-shaped.

*Fig. 8* The Stigmatic surface is a lobed expansion, and when fully expanded, as in *c*, there are three distinct stigmas.

*Fig. 9* Fruit, a Capsule which opens by three valves, and has an elongated slender stalk. Each carpel splits along the middle of its length, so that each valve of the fruit is composed of the halves of two adjacent carpels.

*Fig. 10* Seed, somewhat globular, and containing Endosperm in addition to the Embryo.

## CLASSIFICATION.

*Class*. Monocotyledon.

*Order*. Iridaceæ.
Leaves, long and narrow.
Perianth, petaloid, of six segments.

Stamens, three, with anthers opening outwards.
Carpels, three, united.
Ovules, numerous; Placentation,

axile.
Fruit, capsular, opening by valves.
Seed with endosperm.

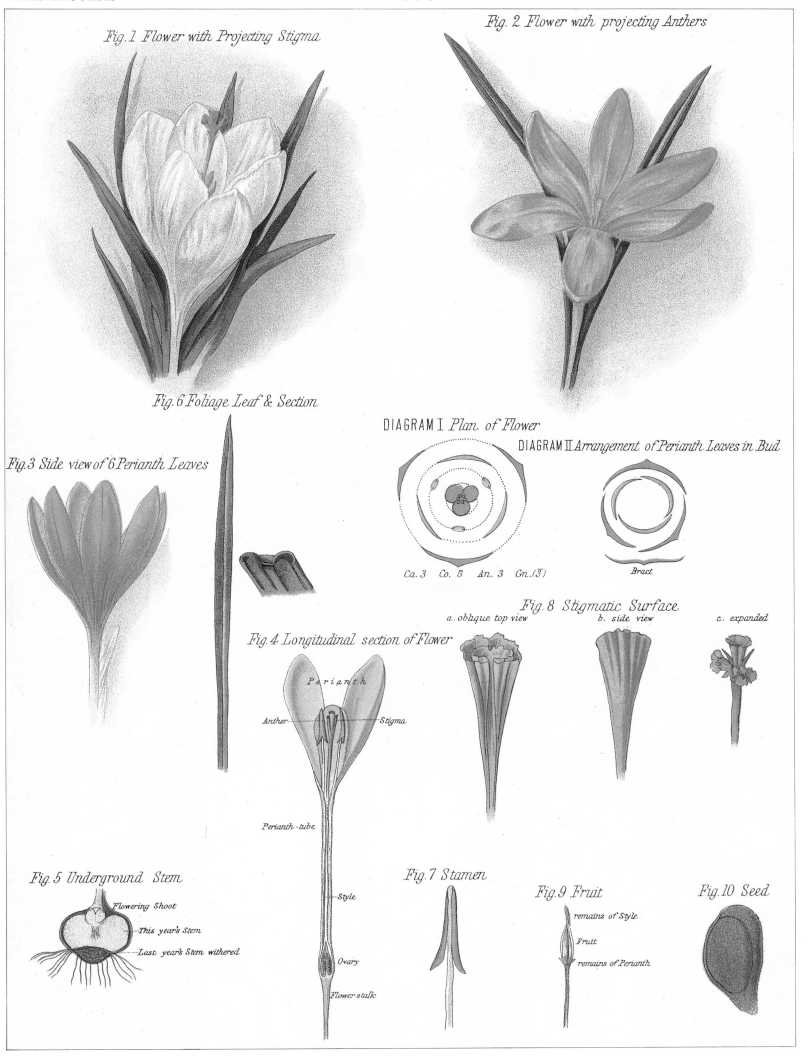

*Fig.1 Flower with Projecting Stigma*

*Fig. 2 Flower with projecting Anthers*

*Fig. 6 Foliage Leaf & Section*

DIAGRAM I *Plan. of Flower*

DIAGRAM II *Arrangement of Perianth Leaves in Bud*

*Fig.3 Side view of 6 Perianth Leaves*

Ca. 3    Co. 3    An. 3    Gn.(3)

*Bract*

*Fig. 8 Stigmatic Surface*

a. oblique top view     b. side view     c. expanded

*Fig. 4 Longitudinal section of Flower*

Perianth

Anther

Stigma

Perianth-tube

*Fig. 5 Underground Stem*

Flowering Shoot

This year's Stem

Last year's Stem withered

Style

Ovary

Flower stalk

*Fig. 7 Stamen*

*Fig.9 Fruit*

remains of Style

Fruit

remains of Perianth

*Fig.10 Seed*

Engraved, Printed and Published by W. & A.K. Johnston, Edinburgh & London.

PLATE IX.
# COMMON ORCHIS (*Orchis mascula*).

Orchids are remarkable, in many respects, for the curious shapes of the flowers, the Peculiar structure of their parts, and the numerous and beautiful contrivances for cross-fertilisation. The common or purple Orchis occurs in shady situations, and flowers early in April. The underground stem is in the form of a Tuber, which in this species is ovoid, or it may be divided at the base into finger-like processes. There are two Tubers, a young one storing up material for next year, while the old one is providing for the present. The young Tuber arises as a lateral bud, growing in size as the old one decays, and thus the plant is carried on from year to year. The flower and its arrangement will be noticed in connection with the Figures.

As the Orchid ends the Monocotyledons, space has been found to show the germination of the Date. The Date belongs to the Palm family, but is here introduced to show the well-developed primary or tap-root, a structure with which Monocotyledons are not usually credited.

## ROOT AND STEM

*Fig. 1* Dig up Tubers at various seasons, before, during, and after flowering, and examine.
The old Tuber is shrivelled, and dark in colour, while the young one is firmer and paler. The relative sizes will vary according to the time at which they are dug up.
Root-fibres arise from the base of the flowering stem, and are thus adventitious.
*Fig. 2* Vertical section of Tuber preserved in spirit.
The old Tuber lies beneath flowering stem, and has been pretty largely rained of its substance to afford nourishment to it, as well as to give rise to the young Tuber.
The young Tuber is now plump and in good condition, and bears a bud at

### DIAGRAM OF THE UNOPENED FLOWER

(*a.*) Orchid—Calyx of three coloured Sepals.
Corolla of three coloured Petals, alternating with sepals.
Andrœcium of one Stamen, the so-called Auriculæ on each side of it representing Staminodes.
Gynœcium of three united Carpels.
(*b.*) Lady's Slipper or Cypripedium is distinguished by having two Anthers, not, however, corresponding to any of those in Orchis, but from their position forming two of an inner whorl of stamens.
A comparison of Lady's Slipper with other Orchids, and a consideration of monstrous flowers, has led to the view that the original type of Orchid flower was one in which there were six Perianth- segments and six Stamens in two whorls, as represented by the

*Class.* Monocotyledon.

*Division.* Petaloideæ

*Order.* Orchidaceæ.

### GERMINATION OF DATE

*Fig. 15* The Seed, or so-called Stone of the Date, was planted in a small pot and kept in a hot-house. In about two months some of the seeds planted germinated, as shown in *b* and *d*.
(*a.*) Stone taken from Date.
There is a little hollow on surface of seed, showing position of Embryo.
Cut through at that spot.

its summit, which is a preparation for the flowering stem of next year. The young Tuber, at least in its early stages, exhibits indications of its first root at the base, but the future rapid growth of the tuber causes this primary root to disappear.

## FLOWER

*Fig. 3* Flower in front view.
Sepals, three, one median and two lateral.
Petals three, the lower one forming a platform on which insects may alight.
Stamen, one, and Anther two-lobed.
Stigmas, three, two lateral and one median, modified into the Rostellum (Lat. *a little beak*).
Ovary, beneath and not seen in this view.
*Fig. 4* Remove sepals and two of the formula Ca. 3, Co. 3, An. 3 + 3, Gn. (3).

## FOLIAGE AND FLORAL LEAVES

*Fig. 6* Foliage-leaf, with parallel veins, and shining surface spotted with dark purple.
*Fig. 7* Bract coloured, with central nerve, broad base, and pointed tip.
*Fig. 8* Sepal, blunt at tip.
*Fig. 9* In a ripe flower insert the point of a pencil for instance, so as to rupture
rostellum, and on withdrawing the pencil, one or two pollinia will be found adhering to it.
Pollinium, consisting of a club-shaped pollen-mass borne on a stalk, with a sticky gland at the base.
*Fig. 10* In a young unopened flower it is interesting to note that the Ovary is untwisted and that the *lip is uppermost* (as shown in Diagram). In expanding, how-ever, the twisting of the ovary

## CLASSIFICATION.

Perianth, irregular, superior.
Andrœcium and Gynœcium, united.
Pollen-grains in club-shaped masses.
Ovary, inferior, one-chambered.

SEED. { Cover, a thin skin.
Embryo, small.
Endosperm, large and horny.
(*b, c.*) Germinating seed—*c*, in its natural position and in vertical section.
One end of the single Cotyledon remains in the seed, absorbing the endosperm, while the other end lengthens and carries with it the other parts of the embryo out

petals, so as to expose central portion of flower; *a* and *b* show the essential organs and their relative positions.
Anther-lobes open lengthways, exposing the pollen-masses, and there is a Connective between, which arches over at the top.
*Fig. 5* Make a vertical section of the flower used in Fig. 4.
The relative position and structure of the parts have evidently reference to the visits of insects. The entrance to the spur is guarded by the Rostellum, in which, as in a cup, lies the sticky base of each pollen-mass.
The stigmatic surfaces project immediately beneath and by the side of the rostellum, so that the upright pollen-mass, when it becomes horizontal on the insect's head, will strike against it.

turns the parts of the flower right round, and the lip comes to occupy its inferior position.
The stalk-like ovary shows the flower to be sessile, and the Inflorescence is therefore a spike.
*Figs. 11 and 12* Transverse sections of Ovaries.
The ovary is one-chambered, containing numerous ovules arranged along the walls in three principal rows.

## FRUIT AND SEED

*Fig. 13* The Fruit has the remains of perianth adherent to it, and opens by three valves or lobes, leaving the ribs still standing between.
*Fig. 14* Detach one of the Seeds from wall of fruit, and examine under microscope.
The Seed consists of a Cover, which is irregularly netted, and an Embryo, which is a roundish undifferentiated mass of tissue.

Ovules, numerous; placentation, parietal.
Fruit, capsular.
Seed, without endosperm.

of the seed. The primary root is developed with its root-cap, and leaves are formed within the sheath of the cotyledon.
(*d.*) The young leaves have burst through the sheath of the cotyledon and the Primary root has become largely developed, giving rise to numerous Rootlets. The primary root has a coil at the base, because it had reached the bottom of the flower-pot.

94

PLATE XI.

# WHITE WATER-LILY (*Nymphæa alba*) and YELLOW WATER-LILY (*Nuphar luteum*).

These are water-plants, growing in lakes or ponds with floating leaves and large solitary flowers. The leaves and flowers are borne on long stalks, so as to reach the surface of the water, and the stalks are permeated by large air-cavities.

The White Water-lily is specially interesting, as showing a gradual passage from Sepal to Petal and from Petal to Stamen.

The Yellow Water-lily has an alcoholic odour like brandy, hence it sometimes gets the name of brandy-bottle.

## FLOWER

*Fig. 1* Flower-bud showing four Sepals green on the outside.

*Fig. 2* Partially opened Bud, halved from below upwards.

Flower-stalk with air-cavities.

Sepals, less green than in unopened bud.

Petals and Stamens apparently inserted on Ovaries, but really attached to Receptacle, which is developed around, and adherent to the carpels.

Carpels with ovaries, partly above and partly below insertion of stamens.

*Diagram* I.—Calyx, of four Sepals. Corolla, of numerous Petals, gradually getting smaller as they approach the Stamens.

Andrœcium, of numerous Stamens.

Gynœcium, of numerous Carpels.

*Fig. 3* Flower-bud of Yellow Water-lily showing five greenish-yellow Sepals.

*Fig. 4* Bud halved lengthways showing superior Ovary.

*Diagram* II.—Calyx of five Sepals. Corolla, of a variable number of petals, often thirteen.

Andrœcium, of numerous Stamens.

Gynœcium, of numerous superior Carpels.

## FOLIAGE- AND FLORAL-LEAVES

*Fig. 5* Foliage-leaf, large and heart-shaped.

*Fig. 6* Floral leaves of White Water-lily, showing transition from Sepal to petal.

(*a.*) Sepal, quite green.

(*b.*) Petal, white, but otherwise resembling sepal.

(*c.*) Regular Petal

*Fig. 7* Stamens showing transition from petals to Stamens.

(*a.*) Stamen, which is essentially a petal-bearing anther.

(*b.*) Regular stamen.

## FRUIT AND SEED

*Fig. 8* The Fruit consists of the numerous carpels, surrounded by a fleshy Receptacle upon which the petals and stamens were spirally arranged.

It ripens under water and afterwards splits up irregularly to allow the escape of the seeds.

*Fig. 9* Vertical section of Seed. The Seed contains a small Embryo with large Endosperm. This endosperm is not only developed as usual in the Embryo-sac, but Nucellus outside the embryo-sac also becomes loaded with nutritious matter, and this is sometimes called Perisperm.

## CLASSIFICATION.

*Class.* Dicotyledon.

*Division.* Polypetalæ.

*Sub-division.* Thalamifloræ.

*Order.* Nymphæaceæ.

Water-plants.

Leaves, usually large and floating.

Flowers, regular.

Petals and Stamens, indefinite.

Carpels, indefinite.

Fruit, berry-like.

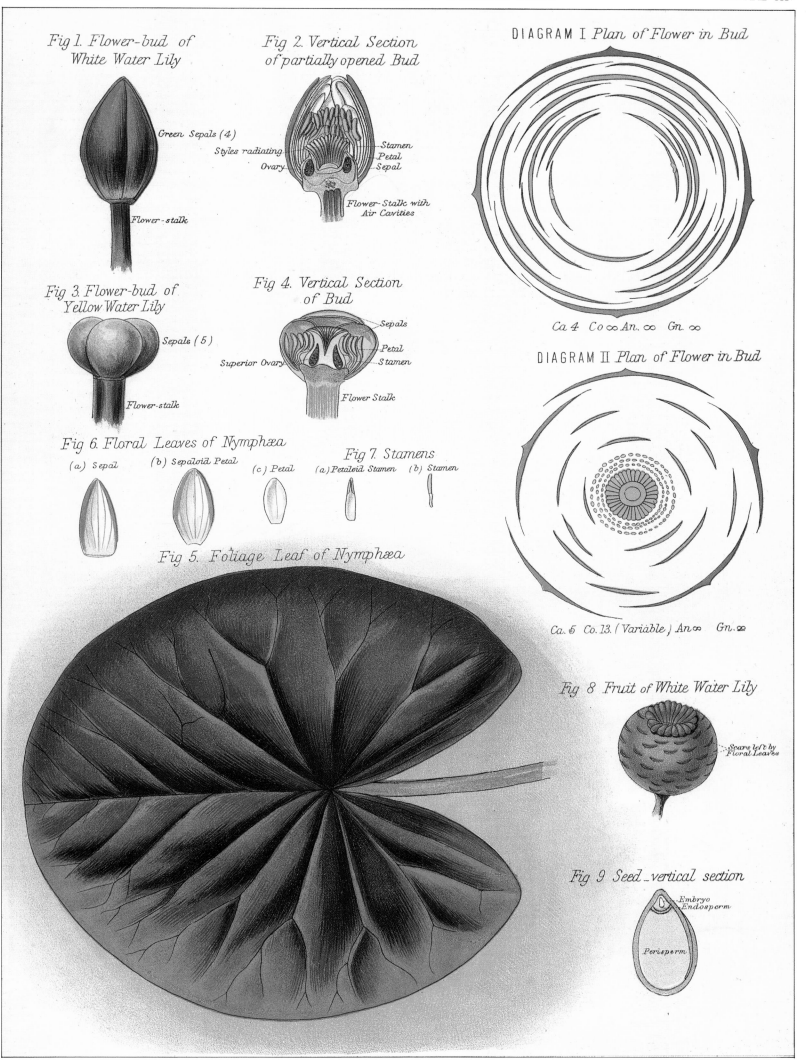

Fig 1. Flower-bud of White Water Lily

Green Sepals (4)

Flower-stalk

Fig 2. Vertical Section of partially opened Bud

Styles radiating

Ovary

Stamen
Petal
Sepal

Flower-Stalk with Air Cavities

DIAGRAM I *Plan of Flower in Bud*

Ca 4   Co ∞ An. ∞   Gn. ∞

Fig 3. Flower-bud of Yellow Water Lily

Sepals (5)

Flower-stalk

Fig 4. Vertical Section of Bud

Superior Ovary

Sepals
Petal
Stamen

Flower Stalk

DIAGRAM II *Plan of Flower in Bud*

Ca. 5   Co. 13. (Variable)   An ∞   Gn.∞

Fig 6. Floral Leaves of Nymphæa

(a) Sepal    (b) Sepaloid Petal    (c) Petal

Fig 7. Stamens

(a) Petaloid Stamen    (b) Stamen

Fig 5. Foliage Leaf of Nymphæa

Fig 8 Fruit of White Water Lily

Scars left by Floral Leaves

Fig 9 Seed_vertical section

Embryo
Endosperm

Perisperm

Engraved, Printed and Published by W. & A.K. Johnston, Edinburgh.

PLATE XII.

# BUTTERCUP (*Ranunculus*) and COLUMBINE (*Aquilegia*).

*(Columbine after Baillon.)*

Buttercups are very common, but they are not on that account to be lightly passed over. The Flower shows the four sets of organs very distinctly, and the parts in each are separate. The Leaves are also very instructive as showing how the much-divided compound leaf gradually gets simpler and simpler as the flower is approached, until there is no difficulty in passing from them to the sepals. In the White Water-lily the passage of one *floral*-leaf into another was shown, but no attempt was made to connect the ordinary *foliage*-leaves with them; in fact there is often a difficulty in doing so, especially where the leaves are compound, for you invariably find the leaves of the flower to be simple. The Buttercup shows the process of simplification very beautifully, and it may also be observed in the white-flowered garden *Peony*, belonging to the same Order as the Buttercup.

The simple flower of the Buttercup has many contrivances worth noticing. It is of a golden colour to attract insects; it has a nectary at the base of each petal to entice them into the recesses of the flower; the outer stamens shed their pollen before the inner, and before the carpels are ready to receive it, in order that insects may carry the pollen from younger flowers, to those more advanced, in which the carpels are mature; and, finally, the whole flower is beautifully spread out to sun and sky, enabling it, with the help of its minutely divided leaves, to get the full benefit of its surroundings.

## BUTTERCUP

FLOWER

*Fig. 1* Halve the expanded flower by cutting from below upwards.
Flower-stalk expanding into Receptacle which is conical, and to which the various parts of the flower are attached.
Sepals inserted on receptacle below carpels, soon falling off. Petals inserted on receptacle, with little scale at base protecting nectar from excessive evaporation.
Stamens inserted on receptacle, and spirally arranged.
Carpels inserted at top of conical receptacle, each with one Ovule, and spirally arranged.
*Diagram* I.—Make transverse section of Bud, just above the base, in order

to cut through the various parts.
Gently separate the parts with dissecting needle and make out their relative position.
Calyx of five free Sepals, imbricate.
Corolla of five free Petals, imbricate.
Androecium of numerous free Stamens.
Gynoecium of numerous free Carpels.
FOLIAGE- AND FLORAL-LEAVES
*Fig. 2* Foliage-leaves gradually passing into floral-leaves.
This gradation of leaves may not all occur on one plant, so several plants should be examined.
*Fig. 3* Floral-leaves.
Green Sepal, hairy outside.
Coloured Petals, notched and unnotched.

*Fig. 4* Filament of Stamen continued along the back or outer face of stamen.
*Fig. 5* Carpel with small point of attachment, and consisting of swollen Ovary, short Style and hooked Stigma.
*Fig. 6* Side wall of Ovary removed, showing single Ovule in the cavity.

FRUIT AND SEED

*Fig. 7* Fruit entire and in vertical section.
Fruit-cover or Pericarp enclosing Seed.
Seed consisting of—
Membranous coat.
Endosperm, white and solid.
Embryo or rudimentary plant towards base.

## COLUMBINE

The scientific name *Aquilegia* (Lat. *aquila,* an eagle), and the common name, *Columbine* (Lat. *columba,* a dove), have both reference to the form of the petals, since one of the petals with a sepal on each side resembles a bird.

*Fig. 8* Section of Flower as in Fig. I.
Flower-stalk expanded at top.
Sepals, sometimes greenish, but usually coloured, hence called petaloid.
Petals with spur projecting below.
Stamens in several whorls above one another.
Carpels inserted on top of receptacle, each with numerous Ovules.
*Diagram* II.—Plan of Flower.
Calyx of five free petaloid Sepals.

Corolla of five free spurred Petals, alternating with the Sepals.
Androecium of ten whorls of Stamens of five each, arranged in ten radiating rows. The innermost and uppermost ten Stamens are reduced to flattened scales, and being barren are called Staminodes.
Gynoecium of five free Carpels, opposite the Petals.
*Fig. 9* Fruit.
Each Carpel opens along its inner

face to discharge the seeds.
A dry fruit, consisting of a single carpel, containing a number of seeds, and opening lengthways along its inner or ventral face is called a *Follicle.*
*Fig. 10 a, b* Seed consisting of—
Cover, which forms a projecting ridge on one side, ending in a *scar* or place of attachment.
Endosperm, large and fleshy. Embryo towards apex, with two Cotyledons and Radicle pointing to Micropyle.

## BANE-BERRY

*Fig. 11* Inflorescence—a Raceme.

*Fig. 12* Fruit—a Berry; containing a number of Seeds.

*Fig. 13* Single Seed with its covering or Testa.

It may be remarked that in Baneberry, where the Carpels are reduced to their lowest number viz., one, the fruit becomes an attractive Berry, which is eaten by animals, and so the Seeds are deposited under the most favourable conditions.

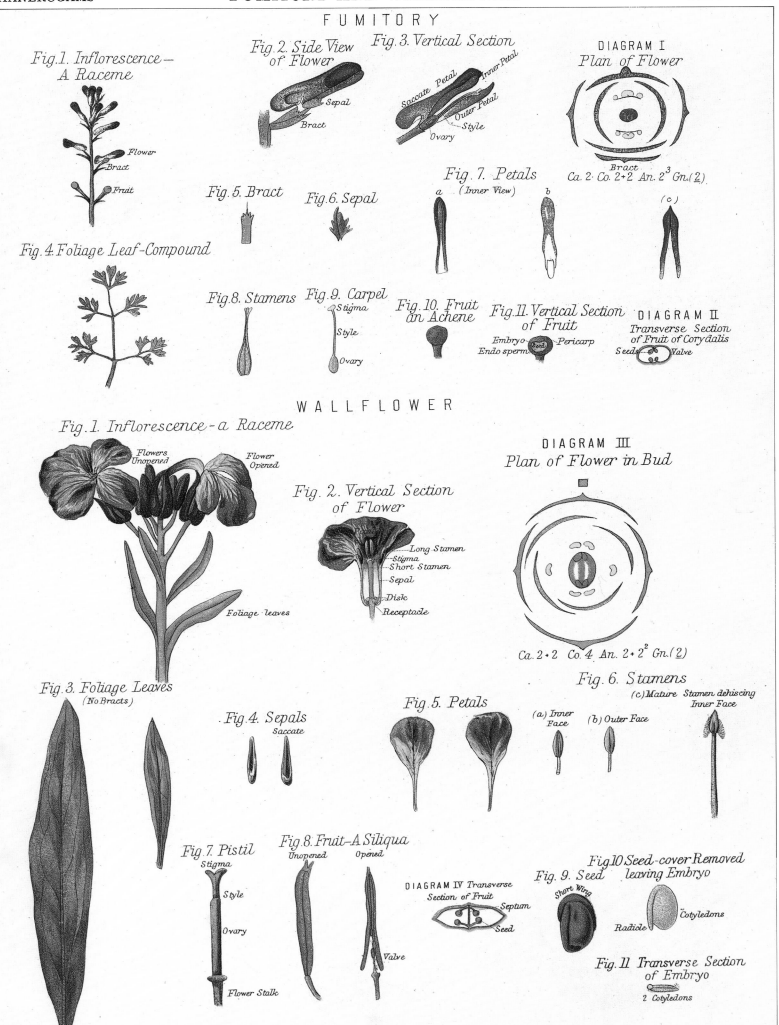

FUMITORY

Fig.1. Inflorescence— A Raceme

Fig.2. Side View of Flower

Fig.3. Vertical Section

DIAGRAM I Plan of Flower

Fig.5. Bract    Fig.6. Sepal    Fig.7. Petals (Inner View)

Fig.4. Foliage Leaf-Compound

Fig.8. Stamens   Fig.9. Carpel   Fig.10. Fruit an Achene   Fig.11. Vertical Section of Fruit   DIAGRAM II Transverse Section of Fruit of Corydalis

WALLFLOWER

Fig.1. Inflorescence - a Raceme

Fig.2. Vertical Section of Flower

DIAGRAM III Plan of Flower in Bud

Fig.3. Foliage Leaves (No Bracts)

Fig.4. Sepals Saccate   Fig.5. Petals   Fig.6. Stamens

Fig.7. Pistil   Fig.8. Fruit–A Siliqua   Fig.9. Seed   Fig.10 Seed-cover Removed leaving Embryo

DIAGRAM IV Transverse Section of Fruit

Fig.11 Transverse Section of Embryo

Engraved, Printed and Published by W. & A.K. Johnston, Edinburgh & London.

PLATE XV.

# CHICKWEED (*Stellaria media*),
# MAIDEN PINK (*Dianthus deltoides*),
# and CAMPION (*Lychnis vespertina*).

## CHICKWEED

The common name of Chickweed is applied to two different genera of the same order—the one being Stellaria, which is easily known by the line of hairs on stem and branches, and the other Cerastium, distinguished as Mouse-ear Chickweed. Stellaria has been chosen for representation which is common on roadsides and waste places at almost any season of the year, and though small it forms a very good example of a large and varied class of plants. The flowers are not very conspicuous, the petals being overtopped by the sepals, and the pollen is ripe before the stigmas are ready to receive it. The inner stamens are often absent, and even the outer are sometimes reduced to three.

STEM AND LEAVES

*Fig. 1* Stem, swollen at the nodes, with a line of hairs on alternate sides. Leaves, opposite, and successive pairs forming right angles with each other. Branches, formed in the axil of each leaf, hence two spring from a node.

FLOWERS

*Figs. 1 and 2* Inflorescence—the main axis terminates in a flower, and two lateral axes below that are similarly terminated by a flower, and so on. Generally when an axis produces a flower at its apex its growth is closed; hence such an Inflorescence is called *Definite*.
When a definite inflorescence produces *two* lateral axes of equal value in this way, it is called a Cyme of two branches, or a *Dichotomous Cyme*.

*Fig. 3* Sepals, longer than petals. Petals, bifid. Stamens, with slender filament arising from receptacle beneath ovary. Carpels, united; Styles, free.

*Diagram.*—Calyx, of five free sepals. Corolla, of five free petals. Andrœcium, of five long stamens alternating with petals, and five short alternating with five long. Gynœcium, of three united carpels.

FOLIAGE- AND FLORAL-LEAVES

*Fig. 4* Lower Foliage-leaves with stalk; upper, sessile.

*Fig. 5 (a)* Free Sepal, with broad base of attachment.
(*b*) Petal, deeply cleft.
*Fig. 6* Stamen, with glandular swelling at base of filament.
*Fig. 7* Gynœcium, with globular Ovary, and three distinct Styles.
*Fig. 8* Placentation, free-central, because ovules are attached to a central axis *free* from wall of ovary

FRUIT AND SEED

*Fig. 9* Fruit a dry, dehiscent Capsule, opening by six valves, and containing numerous seeds.
*Figs. 10 and 11* Seed, with curved Embryo enveloping Endosperm.

## MAIDEN PINK

*Figs. 12 and 13* Pink, in its first condition with stamens mature, and projecting; second condition, with stigmas mature, and occupying position of the shrivelled-up stamens.

## CAMPION

Campion, like the generality of flowers which expand by night, is *white*; since white is a colour which reflects even the faint light existing at night-time, thus rendering objects of that colour as conspicuous as possible. It also smells in the evening in order to guide and attract insects.

In Chickweed, the male and female organs exist, but there is a tendency to reduction in the stamens, and the pollen is shed before the stigmas of the flower are mature. In Pink, male and female organs also exist, but the pollen is shed while the stigmas are not only immature but concealed. In Campion, the separation of the male and female organs has gone further, since the male and female flowers are produced on separate plants.

*Figs. 14 and 15* Male Flower, with ten Stamens—five long, alternating with sepals, and five short, alternating with petals. Corona, at junction of claw and blade of petal, scale-like— essentially a ligular appendage, occupying same position and at right angles to leaf as in Grasses.
Axis of flower, developed between sepals and petals.
*Fig 16* Female Flower, with five curling stigmas, thus offering a large surface for the reception of pollen.

## CLASSIFICATION.

*Class.* Dicotyledon.

*Division.* Polypetalæ.

*Sub-division.* Thalamifloræ.
*Order.* Caryophyllaceæ, or Pinks.

Stem, with swollen nodes.
Leaves, opposite and entire.
Inflorescence, definite.
Flowers, regular.
Stamens, definite.
Ovules, many, and Placentation free- central.
Fruit, a capsule (usually).
Seed, with endosperm.

*Genera.* Stellaria, Cerastium, Dianthus, Lychnis.

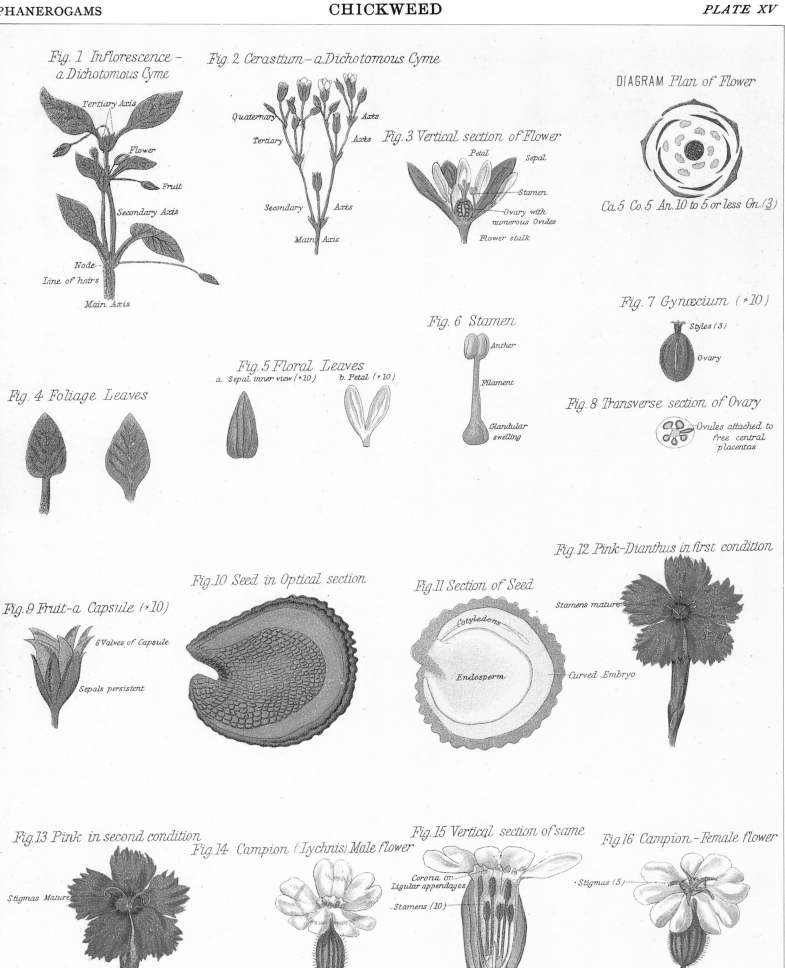

Fig. 1 Inflorescence - a Dichotomous Cyme

Tertiary Axis
Flower
Fruit
Secondary Axis
Node
Line of hairs
Main Axis

Fig. 2 Cerastium - a Dichotomous Cyme

Quaternary   Axis
Tertiary   Axis
Secondary   Axis
Main Axis

Fig. 3 Vertical section of Flower

Petal
Sepal
Stamen
Ovary with numerous Ovules
Flower stalk

DIAGRAM Plan of Flower

Ca. 5 Co. 5 An. 10 to 5 or less Gn. (3)

Fig. 4 Foliage Leaves

Fig. 5 Floral Leaves
a. Sepal inner view (×10)
b. Petal (×10)

Fig. 6 Stamen
Anther
Filament
Glandular swelling

Fig. 7 Gynœcium (×10)
Styles (3)
Ovary

Fig. 8 Transverse section of Ovary
Ovules attached to free central placentas

Fig. 9 Fruit - a Capsule (×10)
6 Valves of Capsule
Sepals persistent

Fig. 10 Seed in Optical section

Fig. 11 Section of Seed
Cotyledons
Endosperm
Curved Embryo

Fig. 12 Pink - Dianthus in first condition
Stamens mature

Fig. 13 Pink in second condition
Stigmas Mature

Fig. 14 Campion (Lychnis) Male flower

Fig. 15 Vertical section of same
Corona or Ligular appendages
Stamens (10)

Fig. 16 Campion - Female flower
Stigmas (5)

Engraved, Printed and Published by W. & A.K. Johnston, Edinburgh & London.

PLATE XVI.

# HERB-ROBERT (Geranium Robertianum).

Herb-Robert is a very common member of the Crane's-bill family, so called from the form of the fruit. It appears in flower towards the end of April, and I have met with it on to the end of December. It attracts notice by its disagreeable smell, and the bright colour of the flower; and in the autumn, when its foliage assumes a tint to match the flower, the whole plant becomes a conspicuous object. The stem forks a deal, and is very brittle at the joints. The leaves are in pairs as well as the flowers, and are deeply segmented. Honey-glands are situated at the base of the petals, and insects entering for the sake of the honey will encounter the stigmas or the anthers at the entrance.

## STEM, LEAVES AND FLOWERS

*Fig. 1* Compound leaf with five leaflets, which are again much divided. The leaf as it approaches the flower is seen to become not only smaller but simpler.

*Fig. 2* Stem brittle at the joints. Leaves with long stalks and membranous stipules. Flower, bent—thus protecting the honey better from being acted on by rain. Fruit, the long and tapering style persisting as the beak.

*Fig. 3* Cut a flower through from the base upwards—
Sepals, hairy, arising from receptacle.
Petals, arising from receptacle, pointed at base and expanded at top.
Stamens, long and short, also arising from receptacle.
Carpels, united.
*Diagram* I.—Calyx of five free sepals.
Corolla of five free petals, alternating with sepals.
Andrœcium of five outer, shorter stamens *opposite* to petals, and five longer, inner stamens.
Gynœcium of five carpels, as shown by the five stigmas, alternating with inner stamens.
Nectaries, in the form of five small glands alternating with petals. If these nectaries be regarded as modified stamens, then the alternation of the different parts of the flower would be quite regular—sepals with petals; petals with nectaries or outermost row of modified stamens; outer with middle, short stamens; middle with inner, long stamens; and inner with carpels.

## FLORAL-LEAVES

*Fig. 4* Sepal with a long awn.
*Fig. 5* Petal with a narrow claw and expanded blade.
*Fig. 6* Stamen with flattened-out filaments.
*Fig. 7* Gynœcium with Ovary, Style, and five distinct Stigmas. There are two Ovules superposed in each chamber of the ovary, one of which grows largely, while the other shrivels up.

*Fig. 8* Cut across ovary to see Placentation.
Ovules attached to a central axis, with partitions between each ovule. This is called Axile Placentation.

## FRUIT AND SEED.

*Fig. 9* The sepals persist at the base of the Fruit, as in Fig. 1, but spread out when fully ripe.
The carpels split from below upwards, and to prevent the jerk separating them entirely from the central axis, each ovary is fastened to the base of the stigma by two silky hairs. These hairs are sufficiently strong to keep the ovaries in place till the wind wafts them to new quarters, so by this beautiful and delicate contrivance the seeds are properly scattered.
*Fig. 10* Seed, smooth.
*Fig. 11* Take the seed between finger and thumb, and make a section lengthways and another cross-wise. Embryo occupies the whole of the seed, and has its cotyledons much folded.

## CLASSIFICATION.

*Class.* Dicotyledon

*Division.* Polypetalæ.

*Sub-division.* Thalamifloræ.
*Order.* Geraniaceæ (*Gr.* geranos,

a crane, from the beak-like prolongation of the carpels).
Leaves, stipulate.
Stamens, definite.
Placentation, axile.
Fruit, capsular

Seed, without endosperm.

*Genus.* Geranium.

*Species.* Robertianum.

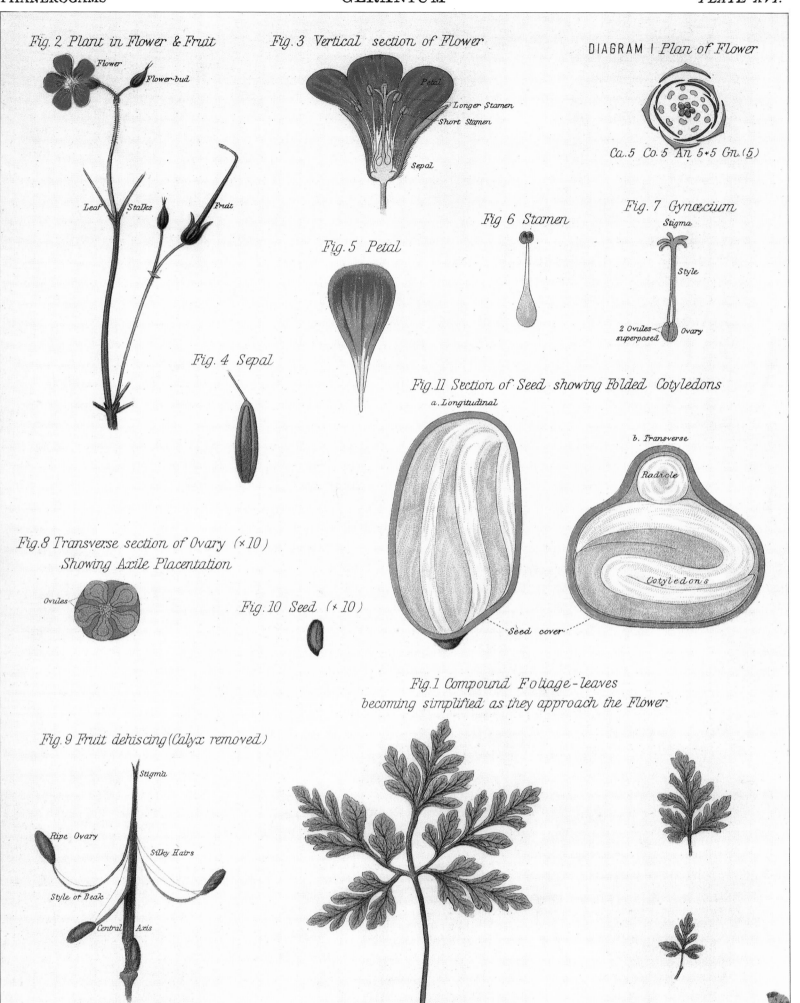

*Fig. 2 Plant in Flower & Fruit*

Flower
Flower-bud
Leaf
Stalks
Fruit

*Fig. 3 Vertical section of Flower*

Petal
Longer Stamen
Short Stamen
Sepal

DIAGRAM I *Plan of Flower*

Ca. 5 Co. 5 An 5+5 Gn. (5)

*Fig. 5 Petal*

*Fig 6 Stamen*

*Fig. 7 Gynœcium*

Stigma
Style
2 Ovules superposed
Ovary

*Fig. 4 Sepal*

*Fig. 11 Section of Seed showing Folded Cotyledons*

a. Longitudinal

b. Transverse

Radicle

Cotyledons

Seed cover

*Fig. 8 Transverse section of Ovary (×10)*
*Showing Axile Placentation*

Ovules

*Fig. 10 Seed (×10)*

*Fig. 1 Compound Foliage-leaves*
*becoming simplified as they approach the Flower*

*Fig. 9 Fruit dehiscing (Calyx removed)*

Stigma
Ripe Ovary
Silky Hairs
Style or Beak
Central Axis

Engraved, Printed and Published by W. & A.K. Johnston, Edinburgh & London.

PLATE XVII.

# SWEET VIOLET (*Viola odorata*)
# and PANSY (*Viola Tricolor*).

The fragrant odour of the one and the brilliant colouration of the other have rendered these flowers universal favourites, but to the botanist they have an additional charm in the beautiful mechanical arrangement of parts for ensuring cross-fertilisation—that is, the transference of the pollen from one flower to the stigma of another.

As there are many other flowers with equally remarkable contrivances it may prove interesting and instructive to ask ourselves and answer for ourselves some of those questions which this very flower—the Sweet Violet—suggested to the mind of Sprengel, who was one of the first during the last century, to perceive the relations between flowers and insects. After examining the flower in order to understand the position and arrangement of the different parts, he asked himself, What is the meaning of all this? and proceeded to write down questions and answers similar to the following:-

I. *Why does the flower bend over?*—To protect the honey from rain, and to place the stamens so that the pollen will fall into the space between the ovary and the free end of the stamens.

2. *Why has the corolla a spur?*—To make room for the appendages of the Anthers, and to hold the nectar they secrete.

3. *Why is the lower petal expanded?*—To serve as an alighting place for insects.

4. *Why have some of the anthers appendages?*—To secrete nectar.

5. *Why is the base of the style bent and thin?*—To enable the insect readily to bend it, as if straight it would be more difficult to bend.

6. *Why is the pollen more powdery than usual?*—To fall out of the anther more readily into the box formed by the  membranous connectives.

The object of the whole contrivance is evidently to get an interchange of pollen through the agency of insects—the honey, the colour, and the smell all being so many inducements to attract them. The insect on alighting crawls between the style and the petal to reach the nectar. In so doing it comes in contact with the stigma and leaves there any pollen about its head brought from another flower. At the same time it bends the flexible style which moves the ovary, thus pressing back the anthers surrounding the ovary, and tapping the pollen-box, as it were. As the anthers slightly overlap, this motion is communicated all round, and the pollen collecting in the lower anthers will be jerked out by the necessary wagging of their appendages. The converging spoon-shaped connectives (Fig. 7) regulate the distribution of the pollen on the insect's head, so that when it visits the next flower, the bulk of the pollen will be left upon the open mouth of the stigma ready to receive it. The lower lip of the stigma will clearly prevent the insect, as it withdraws its head, from leaving any of the flower's own pollen, since the lip will close and none will stick.

*Fig. 1* Leaf of Pansy—Stipules, large and leafy.

*Figs. 2* and *3* Vertical section of Pansy and of Sweet Violet.

Bracts; minute, near bend of flower-stalk in Pansy, about middle of flower-stalk in Sweet Violet.

Sepals, attached to receptacle so as to leave posterior ends, free.

Petals, of different size and shape; the lowest the largest and prolonged into a spur.

Stamens, surrounding the ovary, with little membranous orange tips, and the two lower anthers with appendages projecting into the spur.

Carpels, consisting of swollen Ovary, bent Style, and hollow Stigma, with the opening directed downwards.

*Diagram.*—Calyx, of five free Sepals, unequal in size.

Corolla, of five free petals, unequal in size.

Andrœcium, of five free Stamens, with large curved anthers overlapping one another.

Gynœcium, of three united Carpels.

*Fig. 4* Bract with indications of stipules.

*Fig. 5* Sepal with auricles representing stipules.

*Fig. 6* Petals—two lateral with a brush of hairs, and lower with double brush and spur.

*Fig. 7* Stamen with very short Filament, anther-lobes opening inwards and connective forming a large scoop.

*Fig. 8* Gynœcium with swollen Ovary, bent Style, and hollow Stigma.

*Fig. 9* Ovary composed of three carpels, united by their in-turned edges, which bear the Ovules. Here there is a single chamber and the ovules are attached to the wall of the ovary, so that the placentation is said to be *parietal*.

*Fig. 10* In Narcissus the Ovule was shown on the eve of fertilisation, here—in Viola—it is shown directly after fertilisation. The pollen-tube has spread out on the Embryo-sac and, by virtue of some influence conveyed by the pollen-tube to the embryo-cell through the synergida, fertilisation has been effected and an *Embryo* formed. The contents of the embryo-sac also break up into a number of *Endosperm* cells by a process of free-cell formation.

It may be noted that, whereas in Narcissus only a single layer of cells formed the apex of the Nucellus, here there are several layers.

*Figs 11* and *12* Fruit, a Capsule splitting up into three valves along what corresponds to the midrib of each carpellary leaf.

*Fig. 13* Seed taken between finger and thumb may be readily halved.

Embryo, at the attached end of seed.

Endosperm, abundant.

## CLASSIFICATION.

*Class.* Dicotyledon.

*Division.* Polypetalæ.

*Sub-division.* Thalamifloræ.

*Order.* Violaceæ.
Leaves, stipulate.
Flowers, irregular.
Stamen with Connectives produced beyond Anthers.

Placentation, parietal.
Fruit, a three-valved capsule.

*Genus.* Only one British genus, Viola.

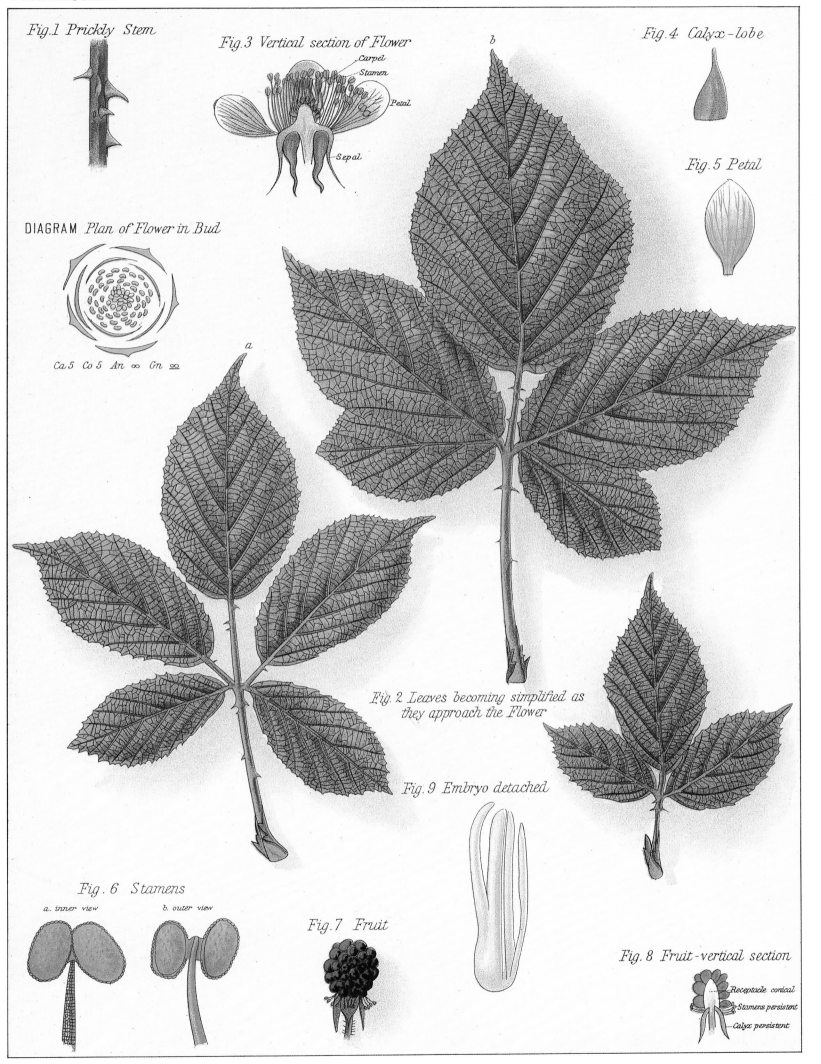

*Fig.1 Prickly Stem*

*Fig.3 Vertical section of Flower*
Carpel
Stamen
Petal
Sepal

b

*Fig.4 Calyx-lobe*

*Fig.5 Petal*

DIAGRAM *Plan of Flower in Bud*

Ca 5 Co 5 An ∞ Gn ∞

a

*Fig.2 Leaves becoming simplified as they approach the Flower*

*Fig.9 Embryo detached*

*Fig.6 Stamens*
a. inner view      b. outer view

*Fig.7 Fruit*

*Fig.8 Fruit-vertical section*
Receptacle conical
Stamens persistent
Calyx persistent

Engraved, Printed and Published by W. & A.K. Johnston, Edinburgh & London.

# PLATE XX.
## ROSE, STRAWBERRY, SPIREA, APPLE, CHERRY, LADY'S MANTLE.

The large and important Natural Order of the Rosaceæ may be conveniently divided into five Series, based principally upon the number of the Carpels and the nature of the Fruit. There is a sixth Series which is exceptional and peculiar.

### I. ROSEÆ.—Type, Dog Rose (*Rosa canina*) or Sweetbrier (*Rosa rubiginosa*).

*Fig. 1* Sweetbriar Rose in vertical section.
Receptacle, *hollow*. The so-called Calyx-tube is simply the end of the Floral Axis hollowed out to protect the Ovaries, hence the sub-division Calycifloræ was founded on a misconception.
Sepals, arising from margin of receptacular cup.
Petals, arising from margin of receptacular cup.
Stamens, arising from margin of receptacular cup.
Carpels contained in hollow receptacle, the stigmas projecting beyond it.
*Diagram.*—Calyx of five Sepals.
Corolla of five Petals.
Andrœcium of numerous Stamens.
Gynœcium of numerous Carpels.
*Figs. 2 and 3* Fruit of Dog Rose entire and in section.
The receptacular cup has become fleshy, and the enclosed single-seeded fruits are Achenes enveloped in hairs.

### II. FRAGARIEÆ or DRYADEÆ.—Type, Bramble (*Rubus fruticosus*) or Strawberry (*Fragaria vesca*).

*Fig. 4* Strawberry flower in vertical section.
Receptacle, *convex*.
Sepals from lateral expansion of receptacle.
Petals from lateral expansion of receptacle.
Stamens from lateral expansion of receptacle.
Carpels, studded over elevated receptacle.
*Fig. 5* Base of Flower.
The Sepals have Stipules as well as the leaves, and these form an Epicalyx or Calyculus.
*Diagram.*—Calyx of five Sepals.
Corolla of five Petals.
Andrœcium of numerous Stamens.
Gynœcium of numerous Carpels.
*Fig. 6* Strawberry.
The receptacle has become swollen and succulent and the little Achenes are almost imbedded in it.
In the Bramble (*Rubus*) the fruits which are little drupes, have become succulent while the relatively small receptacle is dry.
In the Silver-weed (*Potentilla*) both fruits and receptacle are dry.

### III. SPIRÆACEÆ.—Type, Meadow-sweet (*Spiræa Ulmaria*).

*Fig. 7* Spiræa in vertical section—with a few Stamens only shown.
Receptacle a *flat expansion*, slightly raised in the centre.
Sepals and Petals arising from margin of receptacle.
Stamens arising from the flat receptacle.
Carpels, attached to slightly raised central portion of receptacle.
Fruit of five Follicles.
*Diagram.*—Calyx of five Sepals,
persistent in fruit.
Corolla of five Petals.
Andrœcium of numerous Stamens or reduced to twenty.
Gynœcium of five Carpels usually, or more.

### IV. POMEÆ.—Type, Apple (*Pyrus Malus*).

*Fig. 8* Apple-flower in vertical section.
Receptacle hollow and closed at the top.
Sepals, Petals, and Stamens arising close together.
Carpels adherent to hollow receptacle.
*Diagram.*—Calyx of five Sepals.
Corolla of five petals.
Andrœcium from fifteen to twenty Stamens.
Gynœcium, not more than five Carpels.
*Fig. 9* Apple in transverse and vertical section.
The swollen succulent receptacle has enveloped the five carpels now ripened into fruit, and each has a cartilaginous lining.
Seeds, two in each carpel, sometimes one aborts.
Calyx, persistent at the top of receptacle.

### V. AMYGDALEÆ—Type, Cherry (*Prunus Cerasus*).

*Fig. 10* Cherry-flower in vertical section.
Receptacle, hollow.
Sepals, Petals, and Stamens from margin of receptacle.
Single Carpel in centre.
*Diagram.*—Calyx of five Sepals.
Corolla of five Petals.
Andrœcium from ten to twenty Stamens.
Gynœcium of one Carpel.
*Figs 11 and 12* Cherry a Drupe containing one Seed, enclosed within the innermost stony portion, surrounded by a succulent part, and covered by a skin.

### VI. SANGUISORBEÆ—Lady's Mantle (*Alchemilla vulgaris*).

*Fig. 13* Lady's Mantle, entire and in section.
Receptacle, hollow.
Calyx of four Sepals with an Epicalyx.
Corolla, absent.
Stamens, four, arising from beneath disc.
Carpel, one.
The members in this Series are very variable, but generally the Carpels are not more than four, and the stamens are sometimes indefinite.
*Fig. 14* Simple leaf of Apple with Stipules at the base.
*Fig. 15* Compound leaf of Rose with leaflets arranged pinnately.
*Fig. 16* Rose-bud showing the Sepals compound like the leaf, but gradually becoming simpler as they pass inwards to the Petals.

*Summary.*—In the Rose the Carpels are indefinite and one-ovuled, and the receptacular cup becomes fleshy on ripening, forming the well-known Hip. The Anthers and Stigma are mature at the same time.

In the Strawberry the Carpels are still indefinite and one-ovuled, but instead of being in a cup are on an elevation, and the swollen elevated receptacle becomes excessively succulent. Stigma mature before Anthers, hence called Protogynous (Gr. *protos*, first; *gonos,* seed).

In Meadowsweet the Carpels are reduced to five (sometimes more), and the slightly convex receptacle bears Follicles which contain *several* Seeds and *open* along one face.

In the Apple the Carpels are five (never more) and two-ovuled, enclosed in a receptacular cup which becomes much larger and more succulent than in the Rose. Stigma mature before Anthers.

In the Cherry the Carpels are reduced to their lowest—one, and the Fruit, in the form of a Drupe, has reached its highest perfection.

118

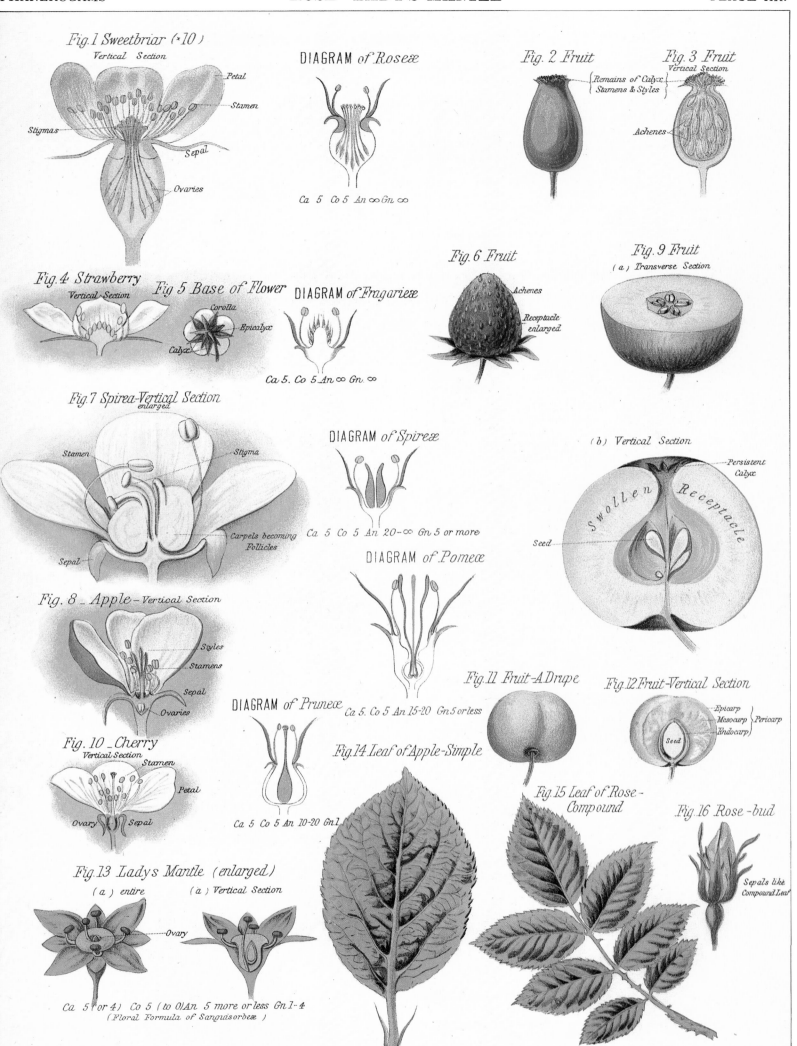

Fig.1 Sweetbriar (×10)
Vertical Section
Petal
Stamen
Stigmas
Sepal
Ovaries

DIAGRAM of Roseæ
Ca 5  Co 5  An ∞ Gn ∞

Fig. 2 Fruit
Fig. 3 Fruit
Vertical Section
Remains of Calyx, Stamens & Styles
Achenes

Fig. 4 Strawberry
Vertical Section
Fig 5 Base of Flower
Corolla
Epicalyx
Calyx

DIAGRAM of Fragarieæ
Ca 5. Co 5 An ∞ Gn ∞

Fig. 6 Fruit
Achenes
Receptacle enlarged

Fig. 9 Fruit
(a) Transverse Section

Fig. 7 Spirea-Vertical Section
enlarged
Stamen
Stigma
Carpels becoming Follicles
Sepal

DIAGRAM of Spireæ
Ca 5  Co 5  An 20-∞  Gn 5 or more

DIAGRAM of Pomeæ
Ca 5. Co 5 An 15-20 Gn 5 or less

(b) Vertical Section
Persistent Calyx
Swollen Receptacle
Seed

Fig. 8 _ Apple - Vertical Section
Styles
Stamens
Sepal
Ovaries

Fig. 10 _ Cherry
Vertical Section
Stamen
Petal
Ovary
Sepal

DIAGRAM of Pruneæ
Ca 5. Co 5 An 10-20 Gn 1

Fig. 11 Fruit - A Drupe

Fig. 12 Fruit - Vertical Section
Epicarp
Mesocarp  } Pericarp
Endocarp
Seed

Fig. 14 Leaf of Apple - Simple

Fig. 15 Leaf of Rose - Compound

Fig. 16 Rose - bud
Sepals like Compound Leaf

Fig. 13 Ladys Mantle (enlarged)
(a) entire
(a) Vertical Section
Ovary
Ca 5 (or 4) Co 5 (to 0) An 5 more or less Gn 1-4
(Floral Formula of Sanguisorbeæ)

Engraved, Printed and Published by W. & A.K. Johnston, Edinburgh

PLATE XXI.

# LEGUMUNOSÆ—SWEET PEA (*Lathyrus odorata*), principally.

This large and important Order is only known to us in Britain as having irregular butterfly-shaped flowers, but in tropical regions the flower assumes a more or less regular form. The Order is thus capable of division into sections:— 1. Mimoseæ—represented by Acacia, or Mimosa—the Sensitive Plant, having regular flowers; 2. Cæsalpinieæ—represented by Cassia—having irregular flowers but not butterflied; and 3. Papilionaceæ—our British representatives—having flowers of the well-known Pea type, with a corolla fancifully resembling a butterfly, hence called *papilionaceous*.

The action of insects alighting on the Pea flower, for instance, may be imitated by pressing down the wings, and the keel goes along with them, thereby exposing the anthers and stigma.

MOSEÆ.—Flower, regular. Petals, valvate. Stamens, definite or indefinite.

| | | |
|---|---|---|
| *Fig. 1* and *Diagram* I.—Calyx of five united Sepals. | Corolla of five Petals. Andrœcium of numerous free | Stamens. Gynœcium of one Carpel. |

CÆSALPINIEÆ.—Flower, irregular. Petals, imbricate. Stamens, definite.

| | | |
|---|---|---|
| *Fig. 2* and *Diagram* II.—Calyx of five free Sepals. | Corolla of five free Petals. Andrœcium of ten or less free | Stamens. Gynœcium of one Carpel. |

PAPILIONACEÆ—Flower, irregular. Petals, imbricate.

*Fig. 3* Compound leaf with Stipules which arise from the base of leaf-stalk and not from stem.
There are two ordinary leaflets, then the next Pair are modified into coiled *tendrils* and the end of the leaf-stalk is prolonged into branching tendrils. Here the leaf or part of it is modified into an organ of support, enabling the weak stem to ascend.
*Fig. 4* The Pea flower in its natural position presents its standard to the breeze, so that it may act as a fluttering flag to attract insects, and as a shelter to the more delicate inner parts. But when an insect alights on the wings which are of the nature of a platform, the wings and keel are depressed, and the anthers and stigma are exposed, but return again to their old position when the pressure is removed. The insect, while searching for pollen or nectar in the staminal tube, will undoubtedly carry away some pollen amongst its hairs and leave it on visiting other flowers.
*Fig. 5* Cut the flower in two from the base upwards.
Sepals, united about half-way down and inserted on receptacle.
Petals—Standard is towards the main floral axis and therefore *dorsal* in position.
Wings, one on each side, therefore *lateral* in position.
Keel, of two partially united petals, is away from the main floral axis and therefore *ventral* in position.
Stamens, one free, rest united into a tube.
Carpel in the middle, arising from receptacle.
*Diagram* III.—Calyx of five united Sepals.
Corolla of five Petals. Dorsal petal or Standard overlaps the rest in bud.
Andrœcium of ten Stamens—dorsal stamen free, other nine united.
Gynœcium of one Carpel, and the Ovules are out-growths from its margins.
*Fig. 6* Petals of unequal size and shape.
(*a*) Standard laterally expanded, and tightly clasping rest of flower at base.
(*b*) Wing with interlocking processes at base for keel.
(*c*) Keel in natural position enclosing Stamens and Carpel, and forming a tight fit with keel.
*Fig. 7* Stamens.
Filaments united for the greater part of their length into a Staminal tube.
Dorsal filament free to about base.
*Fig. 8* Fruit—a Pod or Legume, from which the Order derives its name.
The Calyx still persists, also the slender Style and even the withered Stamens.
*Figs. 9 and 10* Steep some peas for a night in water, when they may be conveniently examined.
On the outer surface of Sweet Pea observe elongated *scar* in the centre indicating its point of attachment inside the fruit, a small opening below, through which moisture can be squeezed, indicating the *micropyle*.
In section of Garden Pea observe that when the skin is removed nothing is left but the Embryo consisting of Stem-bud or Plumule.
Primary root or Radicle pointing towards micropyle.
Seed-leaves or Cotyledons.
*Fig. 11* Germination.
The Radicle has elongated, producing the primary root or Tap-root, with its Rootlets.
The Plumule also grows upwards, producing at first the insignificant small leaves gradually growing larger as you ascend the stem.

## CLASSIFICATION.

*Class.* Dicotyledon.

*Division.* Polypetalæ.

*Sub-division.* Calyciflorae.

*Order.* Leguminosæ.
Leaves, usually compound and stipulate.
Flower, irregular.
Corolla, papilionaceous.

Stamens, ten.
Carpel, superior and solitary.
Fruit, generally a Legume.
Seed, without endosperm.

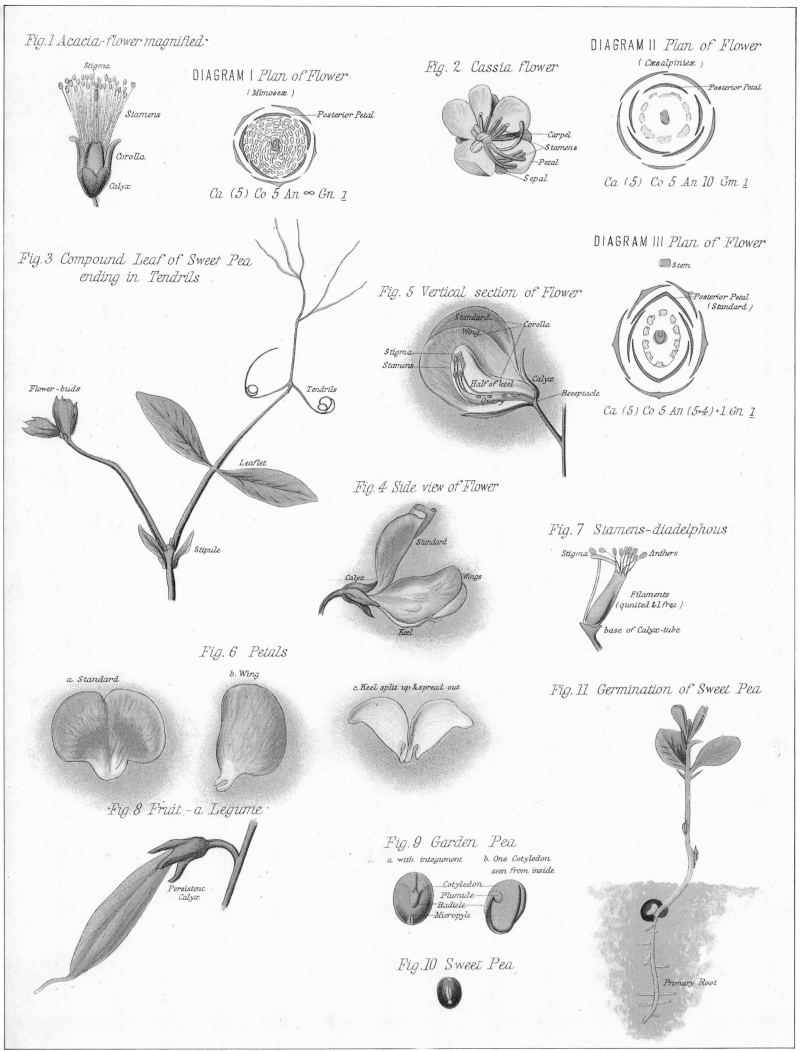

Fig.1 Acacia-flower magnified.

Stigma
Stamens
Corolla
Calyx

DIAGRAM I Plan of Flower
( Mimoseæ )

Posterior Petal

Ca (5) Co 5 An ∞ Gn 1

Fig. 2 Cassia flower

Carpel
Stamens
Petal
Sepal

DIAGRAM II Plan of Flower
( Cæsalpinieæ )

Posterior Petal

Ca (5) Co 5 An 10 Gn 1

Fig.3 Compound Leaf of Sweet Pea
ending in Tendrils

Flower-buds
Tendrils
Leaflet
Stipule

Fig. 5 Vertical section of Flower

Standard
Wing
Corolla
Stigma
Stamens
Half of keel
Ovary
Calyx
Receptacle

DIAGRAM III Plan of Flower

Stem
Posterior Petal
( Standard )

Ca (5) Co 5 An (5+4)+1 Gn 1

Fig. 4 Side view of Flower

Standard
Calyx
Wings
Keel

Fig. 7 Stamens-diadelphous

Stigma
Anthers
Filaments
(9 united & 1 free )
base of Calyx-tube

Fig. 6 Petals

a. Standard
b. Wing
c. Keel split up & spread out

Fig. 11 Germination of Sweet Pea

Fig.8 Fruit - a Legume

Persistent Calyx

Fig.9 Garden Pea

a with integument    b. One Cotyledon seen from inside

Cotyledon
Plumule
Radicle
Micropyle

Fig.10 Sweet Pea

Primary Root

Engraved, Printed and Published by W. & A.K. Johnston, Edinburgh.

PLATE XXII.

# PRIMROSE (*Primula vulgaris*) and HEATH (*Erica*).

## PRIMROSE

The Primrose might be dismissed with the convenient expression, "too well-known to need description;" but, although certainly known, it by no means follows that it is generally understood and appreciated, for in it there is to be seen a wonderful adaptation of means to ends, which Darwin was the first thoroughly to appreciate and to explain. If the flowers are examined on several different plants it will be found that they vary: those on one plant having the knob-headed stigma at the entrance to the corolla-tube, and those on another having the stamens in that position. These two different forms of flowers are respectively called Long-styled and Short-styled. A glance at Fig. 2 will show that an insect visiting the long-styled flower, and thrusting its proboscis down the tube, will carry away pollen so placed that, on visiting a short-styled flower, it will come in contact with the stigma, and thus ensure cross-fertilisation. Reversing the order of its visit, from short-styled to long-styled, the insect would still produce the same effect.

The Pollen-grains, too (Fig. 4), are adapted for their respective duties. In the long-styled flower they are smallest because they are intended to be transferred to the stigma of the short-styled flower, and so have to produce a shorter pollen-tube than the other.

The Primrose appears in early spring (Primula, from Lat. *primus,* first) at a time when insect life is still scarce; and yet so perfect is the adaptation of its various parts to secure cross-fertilisation—with the minimum of waste, so attractive is its flower and scent, and so well-chosen its situation on sloping bank or sheltered glade that it not only manages to thrive, but often overspreads the hedge-bank with its blossoms like so many golden stars.

*Fig. 1* Form and Habit of the plant. The wrinkled Leaves stand out from the base in radiating fashion, and the Flowers also radiate from a centre, having long flower-stalks. Here the Umbel is sessile, but in Cowslip it is stalked.

*Figs. 2 and 3* Slit up a Long-styled and Short-styled form of flower from the base, and compare them. Stigma of one about the same height as the Anthers of another.

*Fig. 4* Dust pollen on slides from the Anthers of the respective flowers, and observe different relative size in each case.

*Fig. 5* Vertical section of Ovary, showing a free central column, to which the Ovules are attached.

*Fig. 6* Fruit—met with in July. Capsule of five valves opening by ten teeth, and containing numerous Seeds.

*Fig. 7* Seed halved. Seed-cover raised into little elevations. Embryo surrounded by Endosperm.

### CLASSIFICATION.

*Class*. Dicotyledon.

*Division*. Gamopetalæ.
Calyx and Corolla present.
Petals, united.

*Order*. Primulaceæ.
Corolla, regular.
Stamen, attached to corolla-tube, *opposite* petals.
Ovary, superior, one-chambered.

Ovules, numerous; Placentation, free-central.
Fruit, capsular.
Seed with endosperm.

## HEATH

Heath is sufficiently common to give its name to large tracts of country where it protects the surface of otherwise barren wastes. It flowers during the summer months, when its modest bloom delights the eye and "sheds beauty o'er the lonely moor." Heather (Calluna) blooms in autumn, and the flower differs from that of Heath (Erica), principally in the Calyx being longer than the Corolla, and having four bracts at its base. Rhododendron is a well-known allied ornamental shrub, with large and showy flowers.

*Fig. 8* Form and Habit of the Plant. The Stem is upright and much branched. The Leaves are in close-set whorls of four, and the Flowers are arranged in crowded racemes.

*Figs. 9 and 10* Flower entire and in section.
Calyx of four sepals and coloured.
Corolla is bell-shaped, with four broad lobes.
Stamens, eight; anthers outside of corolla tube, and each opening by two pores.
Carpels, four, united, with Style projecting beyond anthers.

*Fig. 11* Flower of Rhododendron in section.
Calyx, represented only by minute teeth.
Corolla of five lobes, deciduous and irregular.
Stamens, ten.
Carpels, five, united.

*Diagram* II.—Calyx of four Sepals.
Corolla of four united Petals.
Andrœcium of eight Stamens, four opposite to sepals and four opposite to Petals.

Gynœcium of four united Carpels.

*Fig. 12* Transverse section of Ovary. The Ovary is divided into four chambers, with numerous Ovules in each, springing from the Axis.

*Fig. 13* Fruit of Rhododendron—a Capsule.
The Carpels separate in the form of five valves, the sides of which are formed by the split septa. In Heather the Capsule splits similarly, but is four-valved; while in Heath the splitting of the valves takes place along the *midrib* of each carpellary leaf.

### CLASSIFICATION.

*Class.* Dicotyledon.

*Division.* Gamopetalæ.

*Order.* Ericaceæ.
Corolla, regular.
Stamens, free from corolla.
Ovary, superior, many-chambered.

Ovules, usually numerous; placentaion, axile.
Fruit, capsular or berried.
Seed with endosperm.

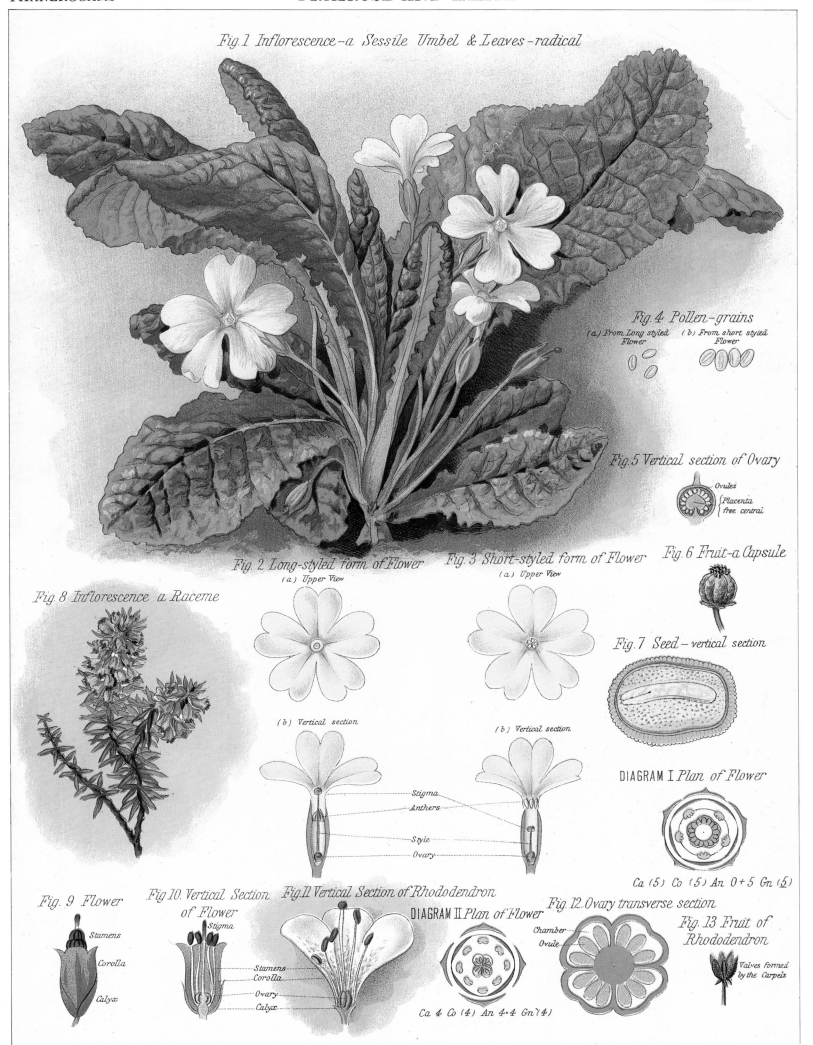

*Fig.1 Inflorescence – a Sessile Umbel & Leaves – radical*

*Fig. 4 Pollen-grains*
(a) From Long styled Flower    (b) From short styled Flower

*Fig. 5 Vertical section of Ovary*
Ovules
Placenta free central

*Fig. 2 Long-styled form of Flower*
(a) Upper View
(b) Vertical section

*Fig. 3 Short-styled form of Flower*
(a) Upper View
(b) Vertical section

Stigma
Anthers
Style
Ovary

*Fig. 6 Fruit – a Capsule*

*Fig. 7 Seed – vertical section*

*Fig. 8 Inflorescence a Raceme*

DIAGRAM I *Plan of Flower*

Ca (5) Co (5) An 0+5 Gn (5)

*Fig. 9 Flower*
Stamens
Corolla
Calyx

*Fig 10. Vertical Section of Flower*
Stigma
Stamens
Corolla
Ovary
Calyx

*Fig.11 Vertical Section of Rhododendron*

DIAGRAM II *Plan of Flower*

Ca 4 Co (4) An 4·4 Gn`(4)

*Fig. 12. Ovary transverse section*
Chamber
Ovule

*Fig. 13 Fruit of Rhododendron*
Valves formed by the Carpels

Engraved, Printed and Published by W. & A.K. Johnston, Edinburgh.

PLATE XXIII.

# WHITE DEAD-NETTLE (*Lamium album*) and SAGE (*Salvia*).

*(Figures of Sage from Dodel-Port, after H. Muller.)*

## DEAD-NETTLE

The common white Dead-nettle owes, no doubt, much of its widespread character to the perfect adaptation of its structure to fertilisation by insects. The contrivances for ensuring cross-fertilisation will now be glanced at. The lower lip of the corolla is expanded, thus forming a platform for insects. The upper lip arches over the stamens like an umbrella, protecting them from rain and preventing the pollen from being carried away, at the same time sheltering the tube of the corolla, at the base of which lies the honey. The ring of upwardly directed hairs near the bottom of the tube will exclude small insects from the honey. The stamens are arranged in parallel series of different lengths, and thus the pollen is not widely dusted over the insect's body, but confined to parts where it will most easily come in contact with the stigma. The stigma, too, hangs down beneath the anthers, and the stigmatic surface is turned outwards, so that any of the flower's own pollen falling down, will only fall upon the back of it, and produce no effect.

When an insect visits a flower of this construction, it alights upon the platform, attracted by the white flowers peeping out from the green foliage; and as it wedges its head into the tube for honey, the pollen on its back is sure to brush against the under surface of the stigma. As the stigma lies lower than the anthers, it will come against it first, and so leave the foreign pollen upon it. When backing out, the insect will receive a fresh coating of pollen from the stamens, and be ready to repeat the process over again on the next flower it visits.

### STEM, LEAVES, AND FLOWERS

*Fig. 1* Stem, square.
Leaves, opposite, and alternately on opposite sides of the square stem.
*Figs. 2 and 3* Flowers in the axils of leaves; the tufts in each axil being a dichotomous cyme condensed.
With a pair of scissors slit up the front face of the flower, that is, the ventral surface, and lay out the parts so as to display interior.
Sepals, separating from each other about half way into long, thin points.
Petals upper lip notched; lower lip with central lobe, and a little tooth at each side.
Stamens, attached to throat of corolla, but their fibro-vascular cords may be traced to the base, and thus their relative position to the other parts of the flower fixed.
Carpels, with forked stigma; the stigmatic surface turned away from the Anthers.

*Diagram.*—Plan of Flower—
Calyx, bell-shaped, of five united Sepals—one dorsal two lateral, and two ventral.
Corolla, two-lipped; upper lip of two united Petals, and lower lip of three (the upper lip is divided in the Ground Ivy, and the little teeth of the lower lip are known in some flowers to grow out into regular lobes; hence, from this and their alternating position, the two lips together are considered five united Petals).
Andrœcium, of four Stamens; two long and two a little shorter (in some instances a fifth rudimentary stamen is found).
Gynœcium, of two united Carpels.

### FLORAL-LEAVES

*Fig. 4* Stamen, showing filament expanding into connective.

*Fig. 5* Gynoecium.
The ovary is four-lobed, and this might be taken as indicating four Carpels without an explanation. There are really two carpels, as denoted by the bifid stigma, which meet by their edges in the middle, and each carpel bears two ovules, thus making four altogether. The midrib of each carpel grows out towards the centre, and becomes attached to it, thus making the double chamber into four. Then the dorsal side of each carpel, that is, the midrib portion, grows excessively, so that the style becomes sunk in the middle, and apparently rises from the *base* of the ovary.

### FRUIT AND SEED

*Fig. 6* Fruit, consists of four little Nutlets
Seed, entirely taken up with Embryo.
*Fig. 7* Embryo, removed and enlarged.

## SAGE.

*Figs. 8, 9,* and *10* In Sage, the *contrivances* for cross-fertilisation are carried to even a higher degree of perfection than in Dead-nettle, as the amount of fertilising material at command is less, there being only two stamens.

In Dead-nettle the two Anther-lobes were obliquely divided, but in Sage they are completely separated (Fig. 9). The Connective diverges to such an extent that this separation takes place, and the upper anther-lobe only bears pollen, while the lower is rudimentary and a mere pad. An insect visiting the flower (as in Fig. 9) strikes against this lower rudimentary lobe, and the upper anther-lobe swings round, dusting the insect's back with pollen. As an effectual preventative against self-fertilisation, the anthers are mature before the stigmas are ready, and on ripening the stigmas come to occupy the position formerly held by the anther-lobes, so that an insect carrying the pollen from one flower will leave it on the stigma of another.

## CLASSIFICATION.

*Class*. Dicotyledon.

*Division*. Gamopetalæ.

*Order*. Labiatæ.

Stem, square.
Leaves, opposite.
Inflorescence, condensed cymes.
Corolla, two-lipped.
Stamens, two long and two short.

Carpels with four-lobed Ovary and bifid Style.
Ovules, one in each lobe.
Fruit, of four little Nutlets.
Seed, without endosperm.

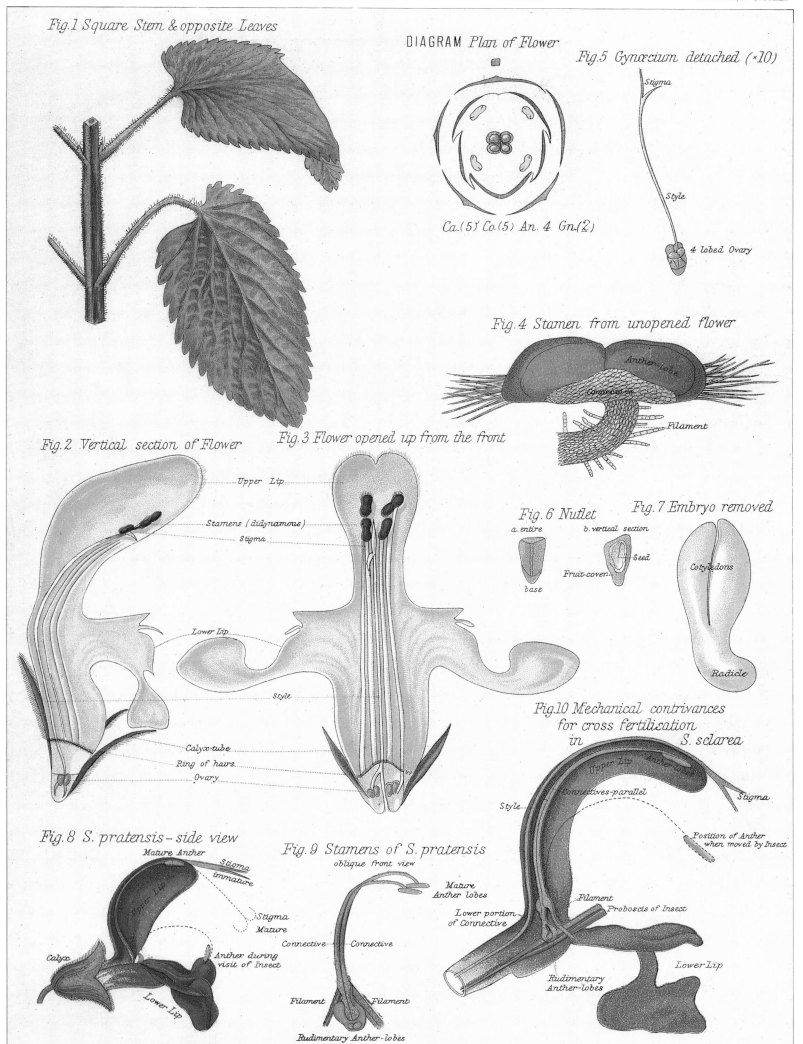

Fig.1 Square Stem & opposite Leaves

DIAGRAM *Plan of Flower*

*Ca.(5) Co.(5) An. 4 Gn.(2)*

Fig.5 Gynœcium detached (×10)

Stigma

Style

4 lobed Ovary

Fig.4 Stamen from unopened flower

Anther-lobe

Connective

Filament

Fig.2 Vertical section of Flower

Fig.3 Flower opened up from the front

Upper Lip

Stamens (didynamous)

Stigma

Lower Lip

Style

Calyx-tube

Ring of hairs

Ovary

Fig.6 Nutlet

a. entire     b. vertical section

Fruit-cover

Seed

base

Fig.7 Embryo removed

Cotyledons

Radicle

Fig.10 Mechanical contrivances
for cross fertilisation
in    S. sclarea

Upper Lip   Anther-lobes

Connectives-parallel

Style

Stigma

Position of Anther
when moved by Insect

Filament

Proboscis of Insect

Rudimentary
Anther-lobes

Lower Lip

Fig.8 S. pratensis – side view

Mature Anther

Stigma
immature

Upper Lip

Stigma
Mature

Calyx

Anther during
visit of Insect

Lower Lip

Fig.9 Stamens of S. pratensis

oblique front view

Mature
Anther lobes

Lower portion
of Connective

Connective    Connective

Filament    Filament

Rudimentary Anther-lobes

Engraved, Printed and Published by W. & A.K. Johnston, Edinburgh & London.

PLATE XXIV.

# FOX-GLOVE (*Digitalis purpurea*).

The purple Fox-glove is a well-known plant, coming into flower about June, and occurring usually on the rough and rugged slopes of the hill-sides. The shape of the flower has suggested both the common and the scientific name. Folk's-glove has reference to its resemblance to the finger of a glove, and Digitalis (Lat. *digitus,* a finger) implies the same. The leaves are used in medicine, and the flowers are adapted for insect-visitation. The Anthers ripen first, and in doing so change from a transverse to a longitudinal position, thus enabling the bee as it enters the bell to carry off the pollen, spread over a larger linear surface of its body.

There are several members of the same Order equally well-known and cultivated, such as Snapdragon, Musk, and Calceolaria, while the Speedwells, usually blue, are among the commonest of spring, summer, and even autumn flowers.

## LEAVES AND FLOWERS

*Fig. 1* Inflorescence—a Raceme, and each flower in the axil of a bract. The unopened flowers towards the top are more or less of a whitish colour, and occasionally the mature flower remains white. It is no uncommon thing to find the axis, under cultivation, terminated by a flower which, under these circumstances, develops its lobes at the margin of the bell regularly, and not irregularly, as in the lateral flower.

*Fig. 2* Take a flower with the lips still closed, and make a longitudinal section, cutting from the base upwards.

Sepals, inserted on receptacle.
Petals, inserted on receptacle.
Stamens, attached to corolla but traceable to their attachment beneath ovary. The filaments are bent, and the unopened anthers lie transverse to the filaments.
Ovary, superior, with a long style lying close to the petals.

*Fig. 3* Take a fully expanded flower and lay open Corolla. Anthers are now open, and instead of being transverse they are longitudinal.

*Diagram* I.—Calyx of five Sepals, unequal in size and united at base. Corolla of five united Petals, the upper lip being slightly notched in the middle, representing two petals, and the lower lip three-lobed, representing three petals.
Androecium of four Stamens, two long and two short. A rudimentary fifth stamen is found in the Snapdragon, sometimes developing into a complete one.
Gynoecium of two united Carpels, as indicated by the two-lobed stigma.

*Fig. 4* Foliage Leaves, long-stalked towards the root, becoming sessile higher up. Bracts, leafy.

*Fig. 5* Sepal or Calyx-lobe, broad base and pointed tip.

*Fig. 6* Transverse section of Ovary (mounted in glycerine).
There are two chambers, and a central axis between, to which the numerous Ovules are attached. The united edges of the two carpellary leaves form the swollen axis, so that the Placentation is axile.

*Fig. 7,* and *Diagram* II.—Speedwell, or Veronica shows a reduction in the number of parts.

Calyx of four Sepals, the posterior one being suppressed.
Corolla of four Petals united at the base, so as to form what is called a rotate corolla. The lower lip is three-lobed, and the upper lip undivided.
Stamens reduced to two.
Carpels, two united.

## FRUIT AND SEED

*Fig. 8* Fruit of Speedwell entire, and in vertical section.
Capsule is laterally compressed, the seeds are attached to a central axis and the two valves separate to allow seeds to escape.

*Figs. 9* and *10* Fruit of Fox-glove entire, and in transverse section. Capsule is pear-shaped, and the two valves separate by splitting from the top downwards.

*Fig. 11* Seed in vertical section. The embryo occupies the axis of the seed, and is surrounded by Endosperm.

*Fig. 12* The Capsule of Snapdragon opens by pores, and the Seeds are curiously marked with depressions, surrounded by walls with jagged surfaces.

## CLASSIFICATION.

*Class.* Dicotyledon

*Division.* Gamopetalæ.

*Order.* Scrophulariaceæ.

Corolla, irregular.
Stamens, four, two long and two short; sometimes two.
Ovary, superior, two-chambered.

Ovules, numerous; placentation, axile.
Fruit, capsular.
Seed with endosperm.

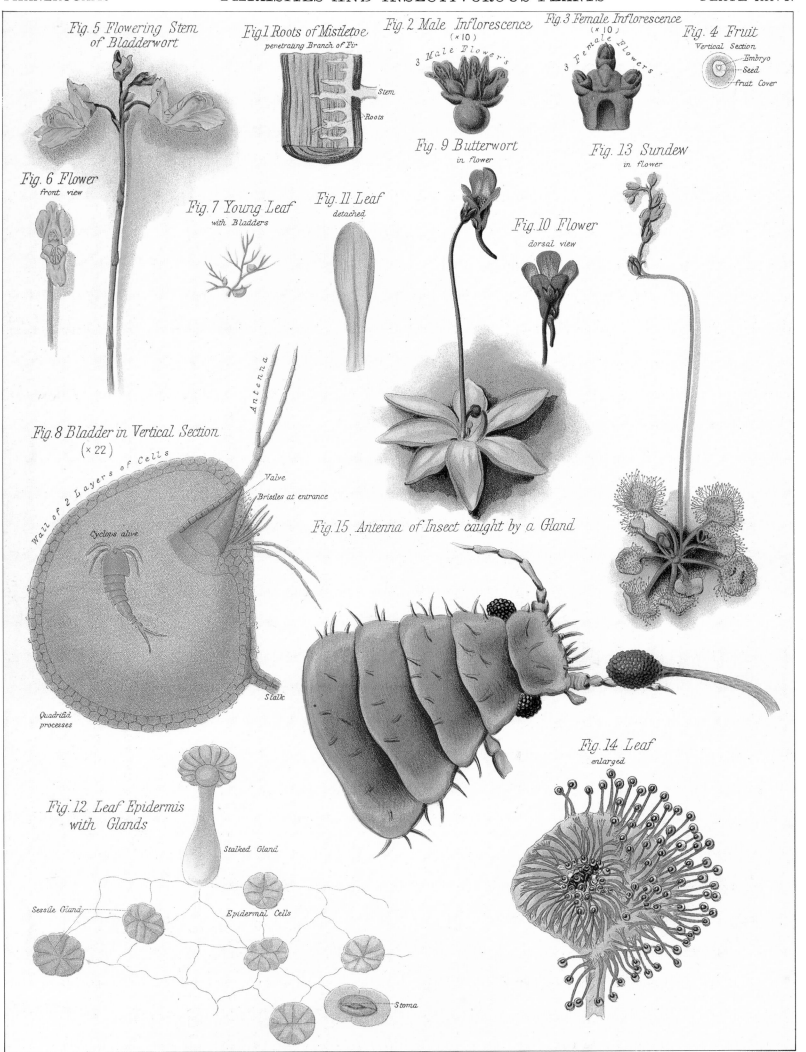

Fig. 5 Flowering Stem of Bladderwort

Fig. 1 Roots of Mistletoe
penetrating Branch of Fir

Stem

Roots

Fig. 2 Male Inflorescence
(× 10)
3 Male Flowers

Fig. 3 Female Inflorescence
(× 10)
3 Female Flowers

Fig. 4 Fruit
Vertical Section
Embryo
Seed
Fruit Cover

Fig. 6 Flower
front view

Fig. 7 Young Leaf
with Bladders

Fig. 11 Leaf
detached

Fig. 9 Butterwort
in flower

Fig. 13 Sundew
in flower

Fig. 10 Flower
dorsal view

Fig. 8 Bladder in Vertical Section
(× 22)

Antenna

Wall of 2 Layers of Cells

Valve

Bristles at entrance

Cyclops alive

Quadrifid processes

Stalk

Fig. 15 Antenna of Insect caught by a Gland

Fig. 14 Leaf
enlarged

Fig. 12 Leaf Epidermis
with Glands

Stalked Gland

Sessile Gland

Epidermal Cells

Stoma

Engraved, Printed and Published by W. & A.K. Johnston, Edinburgh.

Utricularia, but flowering earlier, usually in May.

*Figs. 9 and 10* One or more stalks arise from the centre of the radical leaves, and each bears a terminal drooping, violet flower with a projecting spur.
*Fig. 11* The leaves have usually incurved margins and are embedded in the boggy ground, so that they are on a level with the surface, and creeping things may readily get on to them When plucked up by the root

the leaves soon bend back and almost meet by their tips, and this folding is the same which keeps them flat when growing.
*Fig. 12* Bend a leaf about the finger, and remove a thin portion of the surface with a sharp razor, and examine to see the glands on the surface.

There are two kinds of glands—those which stand out on a stalk and those which are sessile. These glands secrete a viscous fluid, and when small flies, etc., venture on the leaf, the margins arch over them, and the secretion acts upon them until they are dissolved. Here a process of digestion takes place.

## DROSERA ROTUNDIFOLIA (Gr. *drosos*, dew).

The SUNDEW derives its name from the glistening appearance of the fluid drops at the tip of each of the tentacles of the leaves.

It occurs on boggy ground and wet moors, and the moss serves as a sponge to keep up a supply of water. It flowers about July.

*Fig. 13* The Leaves are arranged in the form of a rosette, and the scape bearing several flowers has a characteristic bend towards the top. The flowers are comparatively small, and the white petals are almost enclosed by the sepals, merely peeping forth a little at the top.
*Fig. 14* The Leaf is beset with numerous tentacles, each terminated

by a gland, and surrounded by a colourless viscid secretion. An insect alighting on the centre of the leaf is speedily enveloped by the infolding tentacles, and the copious secretion poured forth by the glands not only weakens its struggles but shortly smothers it. Thus quietly resting on the leaf which forms a trough for its reception, the soft parts of the insect

are gradually dissolved and absorbed by the Leaf, which again expands its tentacles to glitter in the sun and attract more prey.
*Fig. 15* This is a case where the antenna was caught by a gland, and it would appear that the insect is bound hand and foot, as it were, by the inner, shorter tentacles and the outer longer tentacles gradually fold over and seal its doom.

There are two ways in which a plant may feed, either by taking in *inorganic* substances and converting them into the organic material of which it is already composed, or by taking in *organic* materials and working them up into its own substance.

The first mode is that adopted by plants possessed of chlorophyll, or an allied colouring matter. This chlorophyll is commonly regarded as a carbonic-acid decomposing-apparatus; but quite recently it has been suggested that it is the living protoplasm underlying it which performs this work, while chlorophyll merely serves to mask it, and prevent too rapid action in the presence of sunlight. In this case chlorophyll would be an accompaniment, and not the cause, of decomposition.

The second mode is carried on by plants without chlorophyll, or an equivalent colouring matter; and, as already pointed out, *living* green plants or animals may be preyed upon, in which case the attacking plants are *Parasites*; or *dead* and decayed organic bodies may be used, when they are *Saprophytes*.

Starting with the ordinary Green Plants, every stage of Degradation may be traced.

The *Mistletoe* is only partially parasitic, since it bears green leaves, but the *Dodder* is wholly parasitic. It forms little discs in contact with the stem of the plant it has attacked, from the centre of each of which a rootlet is emitted, and penetrates into the tissues of its host.

Then the next step is from living to decayed matter, as in the case of the brown Bird's-nest Orchid, which absorbs the liquified decaying leaves amongst which it lives. The Bladder-wort, too, absorbs the decayed animal matter, putrifying in its bladders.

But a further stage is reached when the plant is able to bring its food materials into a state of solution as well as to absorb them, and this is accomplished by the Butterwort and the Sundew, which have not only beautiful contrivances for catching their living prey but means for digesting it as well.

# CRYPTOGAMS

## INDEX TO ILLUSTRATIONS — FOR COMPARATIVE STUDY

133

# PHANEROGAMS

### INDEX TO ILLUSTRATIONS — FOR COMPARATIVE STUDY

#### "D" INDICATES DIAGRAM

134